LOCOMOTION PAPERS

The
Nelson and Ynysybwl Branches
of the
Taff Vale Railway

by
Colin Chapman

THE OAKWOOD PRESS

© Oakwood Press & Colin Chapman 1997

British Library Cataloguing in Publication Data
A Record for this book is available from the British Library
ISBN 0 85361 512 8

Typeset by Oakwood Graphics.
Repro by Ford Graphics, Ringwood, Hants.
Printed by Alpha Print (Oxford) Ltd, Witney, Oxon.

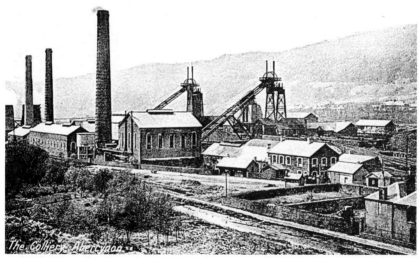

Dowlais-Cardiff Colliery, Abercynon, viewed from the Nelson Branch, *c.* 1910.
Ian Pope Collection

Published by
The Oakwood Press
P.O. Box 122, Headington, Oxford OX3 8LU

Contents

A moment for reflection at Old Ynysybwl Halt on 25th May, 1946.   *I.L. Wright*

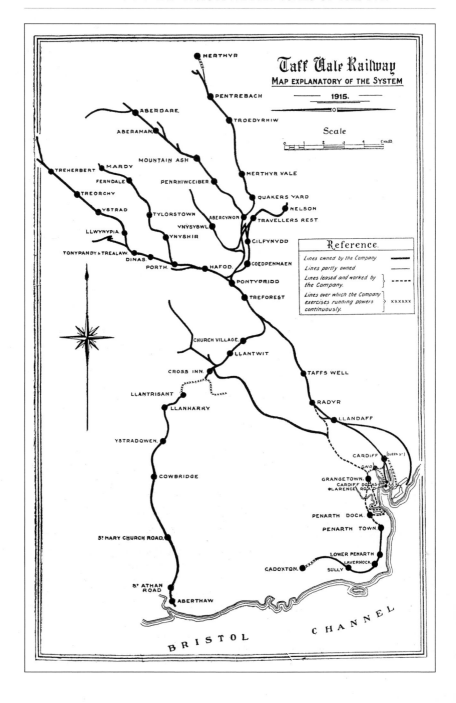

Chapter One

Introduction

For a busy coalfield railway, the Taff Vale Railway (TVR) possessed a surprisingly high mileage of thinly-trafficked single track branch lines. At the Grouping in 1922 just over 30 per cent of the total network of 124 miles was made up of such lines. They were the product of the hectic competitive environment which characterised the South Wales railway scene up to the start of World War I. For most of its existence the TVR was engaged in a desperate struggle with competitors, employing expansionist or defensive tactics depending on circumstances. Such battles often produced outstanding successes, but also resulted in a legacy of relatively under-used branch lines.

Most of these lines were to the south-west of Pontypridd, made up of the various Llantrisant branches and the long rural extension to Cowbridge and Aberthaw in the heart of the Vale of Glamorgan. However, to the north of Pontypridd was another group of branch lines, astride the main line to Merthyr. Originally simple branches off the main line, serving the Clydach Valley and Ynysybwl to the west, and Nelson and Llancaiach to the east, later developments, in the form of various curves and connecting links, produced a complex network of lines filling the available ground between Pontypridd and Abercynon.

The history of the two principal branches - the Nelson and Ynysybwl branch lines - interlocked and overlapped at various times. This suggested to the author that joint treatment in a single study was the most appropriate approach to follow. For a start, the modern Llancaiach branch and the Ynysybwl branch shared the same authorising Act of Parliament, which received Royal Assent in 1873. Both were originally basic mineral branch lines focusing on exchange sidings at Stormstown Junction, but were later to see their orientation changed in favour of the important traffic centre of Pontypridd, at the hub of the TVR system. In this later form both branches were closely associated with the extensive and protracted rebuilding of passenger and freight facilities which took place at Pontypridd in the early years of this century. Both lines also played an important part in the steam railcar revolution that gripped the TVR in the decade after 1903. Their close relationship is perhaps epitomised by the case of Berw Road Motor Car Platform, which, having started out as an intermediate stopping place on the Pontypridd to Ynysybwl service, re-emerged, after a period of closure brought about by the widening of the TVR main line, on the Nelson line, or more precisely the Pont Shon Norton branch. Finally, in the retrenchment of later years both lines ended their days by reverting to short mineral branches off the former TVR main line, with Stormstown Junction regaining its former pre-eminence.

One complicating feature in this story is the changes in the names of the branches which occurred over the years. Up until 1900 and the introduction of the passenger train service on the branch, the line from Stormstown Junction to Llancaiach was known as the Llancaiach branch. The passenger service stopped short of the physical terminus of the branch, at Nelson, and henceforth the line was referred to as the Nelson branch, although this was by no means universal.

The line to the Albion Colliery at Cilfynydd was originally quite separate from the Llancaiach branch and was known as the Pont Shon Norton branch. The extension from this branch to join the Llancaiach branch at Ynysydwr Junction was called the Cilfynydd Loop, but the entire section from Pont Shon Norton Junction was often referred to as the Pont Shon Norton branch. In later years, however, following the introduction of the passenger service, which ran via Cilfynydd to join the line to Nelson at Ynysydwr Junction, the whole line was often termed the Nelson branch.

A similar state of affairs was found on the Ynysybwl branch which was originally known as the Clydach or Clydach Valley branch, with resulting confusion with the line to Clydach Vale, in the Rhondda Fawr Valley. From the introduction of the passenger service in 1890 the branch was generally referred to as the Ynysybwl branch. In its original form the line left the TVR main line at Stormstown Junction, but was later provided with a connecting spur - the Clydach Court Loop - which enabled trains to run direct to Pontypridd. Once again, however, the passenger line from Clydach Court Junction to Ynysybwl tended to be known as the Ynysybwl branch, with the line from Stormstown Junction becoming something of a backwater.

In this study the contemporary names are employed at each stage of development and it is hoped that the various changes will not produce confusion in the mind of the reader.

Finally, whilst on the subject of proper names, it is worth mentioning, at this point, that the village of Nelson originally bore the name of 'Ffos-y-Gerddinen'. The 'Nelson' was an inn in the village and its usage in place of the Welsh name (which means 'Marshy ground of the mountain ash or rowan tree') is attributed to 'foreign' navvies, from the West Country and Ireland who found it easier to pronounce than 'Ffos-y-Gerddinen'. That said, we too may consign 'Ffos-y-Gerddinen' to history and rely on 'Nelson' throughout this narrative.

Pontypridd Junction on 21st July, 1960, with the Merthyr line bearing to the right of the picture, and the Rhondda branch to the left.   *M. Hale*

Chapter Two

The Original Llancaiach Branch, 1836-1870

The spectacular growth of the iron industry of the Merthyr district in the second half of the 18th century lacked one basic ingredient - a cheap and efficient means of transport between the iron works and the sea at Cardiff. Although the valley of the River Taff provided a natural routeway from Merthyr to Cardiff, it was not until 1771 that an Act was obtained which made use of it for the creation of the Glamorganshire Turnpike Road from Merthyr to join the Cardiff District Turnpike at Tongwynlais. Until the opening of the new road, the produce of the ironworks continued to be conveyed by packhorse over rough upland tracks, the historic route, via Gelligaer and Caerphilly, having been improved about 1767. Even though the new turnpike road represented a vast improvement on what had existed before, it soon proved inadequate for the needs of the rapidly expanding iron industry, with the result that pressure grew for a much more effective solution to the problem.

Demands for improved transport facilities led to the passing of the Glamorganshire Canal Act on 9th June, 1790, the canal itself being opened between Merthyr and Cardiff on 10th February, 1794. In 1802 an important interchange between rail and water transport was brought into use at Navigation House, at what is now Abercynon, about 9 miles below Merthyr, with the opening of the Penydarren (or Merthyr) Tramroad. The importance of this location was increased further in 1812 with the opening of the Aberdare Canal, which joined the main canal, just above Navigation House.

To the south of Navigation House the canal passed along the eastern side of the Taff Valley to Newbridge (Pontypridd from 1843) at the confluence of the Rhondda and Taff rivers, and the point at which William Edwards' beautiful single arched bridge across the Taff had been completed in 1756. Midway between Navigation House and Newbridge the main valley of the Taff was joined by that of its tributary, the Clydach. This secluded wooded valley extended for about 4½ miles to the west of the Taff Valley towards the tiny hamlet of Llanwonno, with its parish church of St Gwynno providing the focal point for an extensive and sparsely populated agricultural district.

Although the Glamorganshire Canal was promoted mainly as a link between the iron works and the sea at Cardiff, its opening soon encouraged the development of extractive and other industry along its route. One early centre of mining activity was the Gelligaer district, centred on Nelson, about two miles due east of Navigation House. The Glamorganshire Canal Act contained a clause (the so-called 'Four mile clause') which stated that 'proprietors of any mines, lying within 4 miles of any part of this canal, may make collateral cuts or railways across the grounds of any person, on payment of damages'. This clause enabled branch canals, tramroads or railways to be taken across the lands of third parties, to link mines and other works to the canal, without the need for further Parliamentary powers or the payment of exorbitant sums in exchange for wayleaves. Advantage was taken of this clause to lay a tramroad from

Llanfabon Colliery, near Nelson, to the Glamorganshire Canal, at Navigation House. This had opened by 18th July, 1812 when *The Cambrian* carried an advertisement for the sale of the colliery, together with '. . . a railway from the works to the Glamorganshire Canal for which annual compensations are paid to different parties amounting in the whole to £20 per annum'. By 1819, the tramroad had been acquired by Sir William Smith, passing, on his death, to his son, Sir Christopher. It was subsequently often referred to as 'Sir Christopher Smith's Tramroad'.

Prospects for the Gelligaer coalfield improved dramatically in 1828 with the arrival in the district of Thomas Powell, one of the most important pioneers in the development of the South Wales coal trade. Since 1810 Powell had been working a colliery at Llanhilleth, near Abertillery. In 1828 he took over Gelliagwellt level and the following year opened Gelligaer Colliery, to the east of Nelson, *The Cambrian* of 17th November, 1829 recording that:

> There has been for some days past a very pleasurable excitement among the peaceful inhabitants of this neighbourhood, occasioned by the perservering efforts of Mr Thomas Powell being crowned with the most complete success. This public-spirited gentleman . . . has sunk two shafts of 112 yards each to discover a vein of coal, the existence of which has heretofore been a problem. His most sanguine expectations have been realised; for at this depth he has discovered a vein of coal nearly 6 ft thick . . . Mr Powell has erected two steam engines of considerable power, one for pumping the water and one for winding the coals.

Powell constructed a short length of tramroad to connect this colliery with Sir Christopher Smith's Tramroad, together with tips at Navigation House to enable his coal to be transferred to the Glamorganshire Canal. By 1840 Powell had transferred his activities to the 'new' Gelligaer Colliery, about ¼ mile to the north-east of the 'old' mine, and featuring, as recorded by the Children's Employment Commissioners in 1841, a 'winding engine of 12 horse power for pumping water; coal brought from workings to level by horses, 16 in number'. This was served by an extension of the tramroad, which Powell assumed control of following the death of Sir Christopher in 1839. Looking ahead, for a moment, Thomas Powell died on 24th March, 1863, aged 83 years, Gelligaer Colliery passing to his son, Walter.

Other coal speculators were attracted to the area, following the successful example set by Thomas Powell. By 1835, Sir Robert Beaumont, one-time mineral advisor to the Marquess of Bute, had established Tophill Colliery, to the north of Nelson. This was followed, by 1840, by Duncan & Co.'s Llancaiach Colliery, to the north-west of the village. An indication of the scale of these undertakings can be obtained from the number of men and boys employed in the mines, as recorded by the Children's Employment Commissioners in 1841: 150 at Powell's Gelligaer Colliery; 67 at Beaumont's Tophill; and 56 at Duncan & Co.'s Llancaiach Colliery. Below Nelson, the tramroad passed over a weighbridge at Tai Machine (Machine House), which was used to apportion charges between the various tramroad users. At its peak this weighbridge is said to have been used by 63 'journeys' of 'drams' each week, each 'journey' averaging 48 tons and pulled by a team of six horses.

By the early 1820s congestion and delay were endemic on the Glamorganshire Canal. With its 49 locks in a distance of only 24½ miles, the canal was proving grossly inadequate to the needs of the traffic and a serious impediment to the further expansion of the iron industry. As far back as 1798 plans had been deposited for a tramroad from Cardiff to Quaker's Yard, where it was to divide, one line going to Merthyr and the other to Carno Mill, at the head of the Rhymney Valley, the latter passing via the Bargoed Taff Valley. A branch was to run from the 'Main Line', at Navigation House, to Aberdare and Glyn Neath. In 1823 an unsuccessful attempt was made to promote the construction of a tramroad or railway, on a line laid out by George Overton, from the southern terminus of the Penydarren Tramroad to Cardiff, with branches to St John's Chapel, near Tonyrefail, Llantrisant, Llandaff and Melyn Griffith.

These early proposals foreshadowed the promotion of the Taff Vale Railway from Merthyr to Cardiff. There was a false start in 1834, when plans were prepared for a 'Merthyr Tydfil and Cardiff Railway' by I.K. Brunel, following a meeting with John Guest of Dowlais Ironworks and Anthony Hill of the Plymouth Ironworks. The Taff Vale Railway itself can be said to have been inaugurated at a meeting at the Castle Inn, Merthyr, on 12th October, 1835, of 'proprietors of iron works, collieries and others interested in the mineral and other property of the valleys of the Taff, Rhondda, Cynon, Bargoed and adjacent places, and in the trade of the town of Merthyr and Port of Cardiff'. At this meeting a Provisional Committee was formed to promote the construction of the railway.

Present at this meeting, and elected a member of the Provisional Committee, was Thomas Powell. Powell appears to have been instrumental in persuading his fellow committee members to include, as part of the proposed undertaking, a branch to serve the Gelligaer coalfield. On 23rd October, 1835 the Provisional Committee resolved 'that the branch to the collieries of Mr Powell and Sir Christopher Smith and Mr Beaumont and the Bargoed Vales be made in such a way as shall be determined after a further view of the locus by Mr Brunel'. In November 1835 a notice for a Bill for the 'Taff Vale or Merthyr Tydfil and Cardiff Railway' was published, which included provision for a '. . . Branch Railway . . . to or near the collieries called Lancaiach, near Pontysquire, in the parish of Gelly-gaer . . .' The TVR obtained its Act of Incorporation on 21st June, 1836. Start of work on the new railway was celebrated on 16th August, 1837, when Lady Charlotte Guest, wife of John Guest of Dowlais, laid the first stone of the viaduct over the River Rhondda at Newbridge.

As authorised by the Act of 1836, the Llancaiach branch extended some four miles from its junction with the TVR main line, about ½ mile below Navigation House, to Llancaiach, passing by the village of Nelson, *en route*. The branch clearly had potential for extension into the valley of the Bargoed Taff and beyond, judging by the resolution made by the Provisional Committee in October 1835, already referred to, and by the fact that on 3rd October, 1836 the TVR Board authorised Thomas Powell to employ an engineer to survey an extension of the branch into the Rhymney Valley.

On 11th October, 1837 the TVR determined to proceed with the survey and laying out of the various branch lines, including that to Llancaiach, and the company's Resident Engineer, George Bush, was instructed accordingly. Early in 1838 advertisements were published seeking tenders for the bridge over the River Taff, together with the first 53 chains of the Llancaiach branch. However, it was not until the Spring of 1839 that further progress was made. On 13th March, 1839 the TVR Board agreed to take possession of all the land required for the branch, but to seek tenders only for construction of the line as far as Duncan & Co.'s Llancaiach Colliery. Instructions to advertise for tenders on this basis were given on 10th April, 1839, but on further reflection the Board decided, on 15th May, 1839, to acquire land only as far as Duncan & Co.'s colliery. The contract for this section was awarded to Messrs Storm and Douglas. Mr Storm seems to have given his name to the later Stormstown Junction and Mr Douglas to Pont Douglas, the bridge carrying the turnpike road over the inclined plane on the branch, near its junction with the TVR main line.

Early in 1840 problems arose with the contractors, who had ceased operations, and on 21st July, 1840 the TVR gave notice to Storm and Douglas to resume work on the contract. Evidently, this notice proved ineffective, for on 4th March, 1841 George Bush was instructed to settle terms on which the Llancaiach branch was to be completed with any contractor that Thomas Powell might agree to. Later that month it was agreed that Powell should have £6,000 worth of new TVR shares to be used by him towards the completion of the Llancaiach branch. However, in the event Powell proved either unwilling or unable to carry out these arrangements, and on 3rd June, 1841 George Bush was instructed to advertise for tenders for the completion of the works. On 15th June, 1841 John Calvert's tender was accepted, for the sum of £4,300. Calvert had been responsible for much of the work on the TVR main line.

The TVR between Cardiff and Navigation House was opened to passengers on 8th October, 1840, with the section onwards to Merthyr following on 21st April, 1841. The day before the opening through to Merthyr, the whole of the main line was inspected by Sir Frederick Smith for the Board of Trade. Although Sir Frederick did not inspect any of the mineral branches, he noted that the 'Llancaik' branch was nearly completed. A station was opened at Incline Top, about 1 mile north of Navigation House and about 2 miles west of the village of Nelson, on 29th September, 1841. At its opening the TVR main line was single throughout, the second line of rails being brought into use through to Navigation House station on 1st February, 1848.

Good progress was made with the Llancaiach branch under John Calvert, and on 22nd October, 1841 the TVR Board resolved to give notice to the Board of Trade of its intention to open the line on 25th November, 1841, and to inform Sir Frederick Smith that the branch would be completed on or before 10th November, 1841. However, as the railway was to be worked by horses and was not intended to carry passengers, the Board of Trade pointed out, in reply, that inspection was not required prior to opening.

The completed branch railway left the TVR main line at Llancaiach Branch Junction, and crossed, in rapid succession, the River Taff and the Glamorganshire Canal, by means of bridges constructed with timber spans resting on masonry abutments. It then climbed rapidly out of the valley, by means of a self-acting inclined plane with a gradient of 1 in 8, 600 yards long, to a point high on the hillside overlooking the Taff Valley. From the top of the incline it followed a winding, but relatively level, course past St Cynon's Church, Abernant House and the village of Nelson, to reach its terminus, near Duncan & Co.'s Llancaiach Colliery.

At first traffic on the Llancaiach branch was very light and fell well below expectations. The collieries retained their connections to the tramroad, and it was not until 30th June, 1842 that the first of them, Duncan & Co.'s Llancaiach Colliery, commenced sending out its coal by means of a siding direct from the colliery to the TVR line. The half-yearly report to TVR shareholders, dated 30th June, 1842, noted that traffic on the branch had only totalled 543 tons per week. The reason for this paucity of traffic lay in a dispute between Thomas Powell and the TVR. This issue came up at the half-yearly meeting of the shareholders on 23rd August, 1842, when reference was made to the fact that Powell, in spite of being a TVR Director and having induced his fellows on the TVR Board to construct the Llancaiach branch, was still sending his coal out via the tramroad and the Glamorganshire Canal. About three months earlier Powell had acquired a locomotive which he wished to use on the TVR to haul his own coal. He also demanded a reduction in the tolls paid to the TVR. However, neither proposition found favour with the TVR. Powell's actions were the subject of much indignation at the half-yearly meeting, but he doggedly defended himself with a clear exposition of his personal business philosophy, saying 'I deny any ill-feeling, and candidly tell you that with me the matter is purely one of pounds, shillings and pence. If you cannot draw my coal to my own advantage, I will do it myself'.

This dispute dragged on into 1843; in their half-yearly report to their shareholders, at their meeting on 21st February, 1843, the TVR Directors noted that 'By a reduction of the rates the Directors might have secured a considerable increase from the Llancaiach branch. The Directors have given this subject the calm and most anxious consideration, and have determined it wiser to sacrifice an immediate return to the permanent interest of the company'. However, during the meeting itself relations between the two sides improved somewhat, it being reported that a 'much more conciliatory feeling was manifested than that at the commencement of the meeting'. Following this rapprochement, an amicable settlement was reached between Powell and his fellow Directors, and coal began to flow down the Llancaiach branch in increasing quantities.

Nevertheless, the tramroad continued to be used, in spite of the diversion of much of its traffic to the new railway. On 15th July, 1844 the TVR Superintendent Mr Highton reported that 'the tramway belonging to Sir Christopher Smith, of which complaints have repeatedly been made that the same has never been properly finished since the company removed its position, has been put in proper order'. In particular, coal from Beaumont's Tophill Colliery continued to be moved over the tramroad, although this too was vulnerable to railway competition. On 10th March, 1845 Mr Highton reported that Thomas Powell wished to erect tips at Nelson, opposite those used for his Gelligaer traffic, to transfer Tophill coal to the railway. Traffic over the

" Mr. Powell, another Director, has sent round circulars informing the shareholders that the rates he pays are not low enough. He tells them that haulage and tonnage are double on the Taff Vale Railway to what they are on the Stockton and Darlington, and then adds, with two marks of admiration, that the Dowlais pay a lower rate for waggons by one-sixteenth, or the quarter part of a farthing. He also thinks it right he should go to Cardiff free of locomotive power, because Dowlais does. All these and other complaints he makes, and yet the Lancaiach branch was made at his earnest request, pleading the consequences to him of his heavy outlay at his colliery without the railway, to which he promised his traffic as soon as it was completed. As to the tolls, they may be said to have been his own fixing, and when fixed he pronounced them so low as to ' defy the competition of the Canal Company.' He declared he would use the railway rather than the canal for nothing—subsequently he said he would give 1d. more per railway than per canal. At length the Lancaiach branch is ready for him, and he has a speedy conveyance to Cardiff 4¾d. per ton cheaper than the canal, and then he goes by the canal because the railway rates are not low enough. He puts out a circular to explain his conduct and enforce his complaints. He tells the shareholders of doubled charges on the Taff Vale Railway, and is silent as to a nine-fold charge on the Stockton and Darlington, on which road all the coal pays 9d. at an incline. Mr. Powell has one incline to pay at, and the charge is 1d., and while he keeps the 9d. out of sight he dwells with astonishment on the discrepancy relating to the fourth part of a farthing."

Extract from statement of case produced by Committee of Inquiry appointed by TVR shareholders, 17th May, 1843.

tramroad declined as more use was made of the railway, and it gradually fell into disuse. In March 1864 it was reported that the section from St Cynon's Church to Abernant House was about to be converted into a 'good road for public traffic'.

In late 1845, at the peak of the first Railway Mania, the TVR found itself threatened on all sides by projected railways. On 16th September, 1845 the TVR entered into the spirit of the age, when instructions were given to make surveys of the 'various valleys which fall into the Taff', including the Rhondda, the Clydach and the Bargoed Taff, as far as Bedlinog. In the event the TVR did not make a detailed survey of the Bargoed Taff Valley, and the proposal was limited to an extension of the Llancaiach branch as far as the terminus originally authorised by the TVR Act of 1836.

Although nothing came of this particular proposal, the prospect of an extension of the Llancaiach branch re-emerged in June 1853, when the promoters of the Rhymney Railway (RR) approached the TVR seeking assistance with their proposed railway. At first, the TVR responded positively to this suggestion, but by October 1853 relations had cooled somewhat and the Rhymney promoters were informed that the TVR was not prepared to offer any pecuniary assistance towards the proposed railway, nor was the company willing to commit itself to altering the inclined plane on the Llancaiach branch.

The plans for the RR, deposited in November 1853, envisaged an extension of the Llancaiach Branch, via Hengoed, to the Rhymney Iron Works, at the head of the Rhymney Valley, with a branch up the Bargoed Rhymney Valley and a connection to the authorised Taff Vale Extension of the Newport Abergavenny and Hereford Railway (NA&HR), at Hengoed. In addition, a deviation of the Llancaiach branch was proposed, in order to avoid the use of the inclined plane. By this date the attitude of the TVR had moved from one of tempered support, through acquiescence and indifference, to outright hostility: on 29th December, 1853 the TVR Board determined to oppose the Rhymney Railway in Parliament. In the wake of this opposition, the inclined plane deviation line and junction with the TVR were struck out of the Bill, and the RR Act, which received Royal Assent on 24th July, 1854, was confined to a line from Rhymney to Hengoed (junction with the NA&HR), with a branch into the Bargoed Rhymney Valley. Such a truncated version of the scheme did not satisfy the promoters, however, and on 2nd July, 1855 a further Act was obtained authorising the extension of the RR from Hengoed to a junction with the TVR at Walnut Tree Bridge, near Taffs Well. The section from Rhymney to Hengoed opened to goods and mineral traffic on 28th December, 1857, and from Hengoed to Walnut Tree Bridge on 25th February, 1858. A passenger service was introduced between Cardiff and Rhymney on 31st March, 1858.

Another unsuccessful proposal for the extension of the Llancaiach branch was made in 1854, when plans were deposited for the Taff Bargoed Railway, from the terminus of the branch into the Bargoed Taff Valley, as far as Bryn Caerau Farmhouse, near Fochriw, together with a deviation line to avoid the inclined plane.

By the mid-1850s traffic on the Llancaiach branch had grown significantly, with patterns of movement becoming much more complex. At first, coal had

TŶ HILL COLLIERY, parish of Gelligaer, Glamorganshire.—*Robert Beaumont, Esq.*, of Llanduff, Occupier.

Males employed:—

Adults 50
Under 18 years of age 11
Under 13 years of age 6

Coal brought by horses from the workings on railed roads; longest road three-fourths of a mile; dip and rise 3 inches in 24; no air-doors; no fire-damp, but much choke-damp.

No. 144. Mr. *Jonathan Isaacs*:

There are about 70 persons employed at this colliery. I am not the appointed agent, but in the absence of Mr. Beaumont I pay the men, and make up all the accounts. I have kept a smithy here some years, and am well acquainted with the habits and condition of the colliers of this locality. We have no sinking, as we draw the coals from the level. Air-doors are not necessary in this work, as there is no fire-damp; there is some little choke-damp in this and the other pits in the neighbourhood, and many men suffer from the asthma which it creates at the age of from 35 to 40. The colliers in this neighbourhood, upon the whole, are pretty healthy, but I think the rising generation not likely to be so, from the curly age at which they are taken into mines.

I have noticed that the children of miners who are sent to work do not grow as they would do; they get pale in their looks, and are thin and weak in their limbs; any one can distinguish a collier's child from the children of other working people. There is a total absence of education in this neighbourhood, and the people do not seem to care much about it. The wives are very clean in their dwellings, and the girls, who generally stay at home to nurse the children or to fetch water, are like the males of the neighbourhood very ignorant. I should think not one in ten can read, and not five in our colliery can read English.

LLANCAYACH COLLIERY, parish of Gelligaer, Glamorganshire.—Messrs. *Duncan and Co.*, Occupiers.

Males employed:—

Adults 40
Under 18 years of age 10
Under 13 years of age 6

Steam-power 24 horses; winding-engine raises coal 60 yards, to a level 24 yards below the surface; coals brought from the workings to the pit-bottom by horses.

No. 152. Mr. *Richard Andrews*, overseer:

Colliers take their children to work below ground at very early ages. There is one little fellow, by name John Davis, helping his father, who is certainly not more than five years old. It is not unfrequent for colliers here to take them down, even in petticoats, to claim a dram. The effect of taking children down so young has a very bad influence on their health. In the first place they are half starved below, as they never can get their meat like other people, and they never grow like other children; as to education, it is quite out of the question.

No lad can be thoroughly useful till he is 13 or 14 years of age; and it is poverty or dissipation which causes men thus to deprive their children of light and air. At this work nearly half the men can read Welsh, but very few of them can read English, which keeps them all dark; but the wives and daughters are excessively ignorant.

The girls are sent to work at farm-houses at 10 and 12 years of age. They get their food for their labour for two or three years, and afterwards from 40s. to 60s. a-year. I see no difference between the agriculturists and the colliers of this quarter; there may, indeed, be a shade of difference in the intelligence of the two classes in favour of the colliers. There are very few cases of bastiardy or desertion, as it is customary amongst the men to marry when the woman is pregnant, or when the first child is delivered. The miners about here are very subject to asthmatic complaints and to rheumatism, arising from the quantity of water in the pits; most of them have large families.

GELLIGAER COLLIERY, parish of Gelligaer, Glamorganshire.—Messrs. *Powell and Co.*, Occupiers.

Number of persons employed:—

Adults 127
Under 18 years of age 13
Under 13 years of age 10

Winding-engine of 12-horse power for pumping water; coal brought from workings to level by horses, 16 in number; boys employed as horse-drivers, and air-door keepers, and filling coal; main-roads six feet high, present working-seam five feet thick.

No. 137. Mr. *William Jenkins*, clerk and under-agent to Gelligaer Colliery:

Been some years at these works, and am well acquainted with the working population of the district. Coal-working has attracted a large number of colliers to this spot from neighbouring counties, most of whom, so far as regards moral or religious knowledge, are in a deplorably low state. I should think that out of the adults we employ not one in ten can read, and certainly not more than six of the whole number can read well; and as the children are taken down as soon as they can crawl, even in petticoats, ignorance is perpetuated. The people though ignorant are of very peaceable habits as a mass. In this part there are more colliers than can get full employ, but they all act in union as to keeping up wages. In consequence of the low price of coal last year we were obliged to reduce the price of working coal from 2s. to 1s. 10d., and all stuck out from the 1st of June to the 12th of August, 1840, when they returned to their work, on entering into an agreement with the masters to work coal on a graduated scale, that scale to be regulated by the price coal sold for at Cardiff. Soon after, a fall of 3d. per ton took place in consequence of reduced prices, to which the men readily assented, and now, as the price had increased, 2d. per ton had been added, and the working prices are, in this place, 1s. 6d. to 1s. 8d. per ton, and the men usually cut down 15 to 16 tons weekly, working, upon an average, 10 hours daily. The colliers about this part are stationary, and the only discontents that arise from the high prices of provisions operating on their present reduced wages. The wages of other men in this quarter are not equally reduced. Masons, good workmen, get 4s. 6d. a-day of 12 hours, but the average of colliers is under 3s. at the present. It is expected that all labourers' wages will be reduced about this quarter. We have given notice of a reduction to all our carpenters, smiths, and day-labourers. The farm-labourers and others are quite as uneducated as our colliers, and I think far less intelligent.

Children taken down by miners lose their strength and hale appearance. It is a pity to see the little things carried in so early. The youngest that we have is John Howell; he is about seven years old, and, as near as I recollect, been below seven or eight months. Schooling is out of the question, there not having been a schoolmaster in the village for some time till the last four months. Only one accident within two years, Richard Richards *killed* by coal falling from roof. Men belonging to Odd Fellow societies, and Ivorites who support each other in sickness.

Extract from Appendix to First Report of Children's Employment Commissioners, 1842.

moved mainly from pit to sea, but in January 1855 it was reported that Duncan & Co. were taking blackband ironstone from Llancaiach to Dowlais, while Thomas Powell and Mr Cartwright (who had acquired Tophill Colliery) were sending coal to various ironworks. There was often serious congestion on the branch. Thomas Powell, who at this date owned some 460 wagons, was in the habit, when short of orders for steam coal, of sending all his surplus wagons to the Llancaiach branch for house coal, thereby taking up all the spare siding room in the process.

As far back as 1847, the NA&HR had obtained an Act authorising the construction of its Taff Vale Extension (TVE), from Pontypool Road to join the TVR at Quaker's Yard. The TVE included some very heavy engineering, the outstanding example being Crumlin viaduct, and the line was opened in stages between 1855 and 1858. It was not until 5th January, 1858 that the last section, from Tredegar Junction (Pontllanfraith) through Llancaiach to Quaker's Yard was opened to passengers. With the opening of Quaker's Yard the TVR closed its nearby Incline Top station to passengers, a move which did not prove popular with the residents of the Llanfabon and Nelson districts, for whom Incline Top, despite its very basic facilities, was much more convenient than Quaker's Yard. On 4th February, 1859, George Fisher reported that a Memorial had been received from the inhabitants of Llanfabon and its neighbourhood pressing for the re-opening of Incline Top station. In recommending the rejection of this request, Fisher noted that there was no public road to the former station, that the men employed at Incline Top were constantly engaged with the stationary engine and machinery, and that the distance from there to Quaker's Yard station was only about ½ mile.

The TVE through Llancaiach was originally only single track, but was doubled in 1863. Just south of Llancaiach Colliery, it crossed the Llancaiach branch on the level, a feature which caused some concern to the Board of Trade Inspector, until additional safety appliances were installed. Two other level crossings existed where the TVE crossed the lines to Tophill and Gelligaer Collieries. A station was provided on the TVE at Llancaiach, hemmed in between the Llancaiach and Tophill crossings. The booking office at this station was destroyed by fire on 6th January, 1868.

In the 1858 Parliamentary Session the NA&HR sought powers, through the medium of a Bill for the 'Merthyr Junction Railway' for an independent line from Quaker's Yard to Merthyr. This Bill was withdrawn, following an agreement, dated 13th February, 1858, between the NA&HR and the TVR, which, amongst other things, gave the TVR running powers over the TVE between Llancaiach and Quaker's Yard. Similar powers were granted to the NA&HR in respect of the section of the TVR main line from Quaker's Yard to Merthyr, including the running of two passenger trains, each way, each day over this section. On 1st March, 1858 the NA&HR took advantage of these powers by extending certain trains over the TVR between Quaker's Yard and Merthyr.

The opening of the TVE ended the TVR's isolation from the standard gauge network which had grown up between the Midlands and south-east Wales. In 1857, in anticipation of this development, the TVR had carried out extensive alterations throughout its system to enable its trains to run on the left-hand line

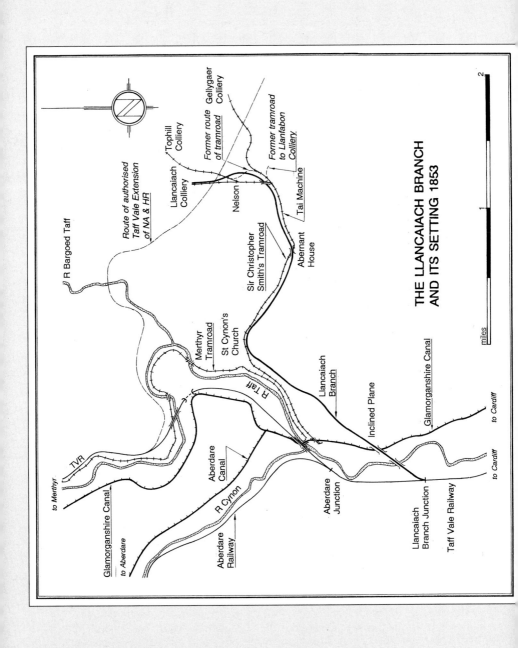

THE LLANCAIACH BRANCH
AND ITS SETTING 1853

of rails instead of the right-hand, as had been the case up until then.

The connection between the TVE and the TVR main line at Quaker's Yard introduced the prospect of an alternative route for Llancaiach coal, avoiding the rope-worked incline on the Llancaiach branch, near the junction with the main line. However, the potential of such a route was undermined by the presence of the Main Incline on the TVR main line between Aberdare Junction and Quaker's Yard. In order to overcome the dramatic change of levels between these two points, Brunel had resorted to the contemporary expedient of an inclined plane, worked by a stationary steam engine. This also enabled relatively easy gradients to be achieved on the rest of the main line. The incline itself was 880 yards long and comprised two equal sections at 1 in 20¾ and 1 in 18. In the early days, the Main Incline did not prove an undue hindrance, as the TVR was able to charge an additional toll for services performed at the incline. However, with the opening of the TVE, coal traffic from the Rhondda and Aberdare Valleys, destined for London, Birkenhead and the Midland Counties, via Quaker's Yard and Pontypool Road, became an important and rapidly growing feature. By 1864 this traffic had grown to the extent that the Main Incline was in use for 18 to 20 hours of each day. The opening of the GWR line between Quaker's Yard and the TVR at Mountain Ash and the Aberdare Valley Railway at Middle Duffryn in that year provided a direct route for traffic from the Aberdare Valley, but the growth of the Rhondda trade alone threatened to overwhelm the incline.

On 17th March, 1864 George Fisher, Engineer and General Superintendent of the TVR, produced a lengthy report on the case for replacing the Main Incline with a more easily graded route. Powers for such a deviation had been obtained in 1857, but this did not necessarily imply early action as the Act contained a number of far-sighted proposals, such as powers for widening the TVR main line to four tracks, which were not implemented for many years. Fisher had become convinced of the need to replace the Main Incline, but his report also dealt with the implications of the agreement with the NA&HR of 13th February, 1858, and the question of TVR running powers between Llancaiach and Quaker's Yard. He clearly foresaw the likely course of events when he commented: 'assuming the Main Incline altered, I consider it more than probable that all traffic now worked over the Llancaiach branch would be brought via Quaker's Yard Junction with advantage to the freighters and to this company'.

With traffic growing all the time and competitors eager to step in to take advantage of any perceived deficiency, the continued existence of such an obsolete feature as the Main Incline had become a serious risk in relation to the future well-being of the TVR.

The Directors, therefore, were faced with a clear choice, and having considered Fisher's forceful arguments at their meeting on 18th March, 1864, they set aside their natural prejudice against additional capital expenditure and agreed to the replacement of the inclined plane with a more easily graded alignment suitable for locomotive haulage. The new line was built alongside the old to a gradient of 1 in 40. It opened in mid-1867 and brought about a substantial improvement to the route used by the Rhondda coal traffic between

Pontypridd and Quaker's Yard for interchange with the TVE line. This route was improved further in October 1872 with the opening of the North Curve at Pontypridd, whereby trains from the Rhondda Valleys could pass directly to the Merthyr line, without the need for reversal at Pontypridd.

The GWR (Various Powers) Act 1867 gave statutory authority to the TVR's running powers between Quaker's Yard and Llancaiach. The Act also required the GWR to give consent to the formation of a junction between the TVE line and the Llancaiach branch, at Llancaiach, if requested by the TVR. On 25th September, 1868 a meeting took place between William Done Bushell, Resident Director (i.e. Managing Director) of the TVR and Joshua Williams, South Wales divisional manager of the GWR, at the TVR's office in Cardiff, at which agreement was reached on the following points:

1. The three level crossings at Llancaiach were to be dispensed with.
2. Sidings were to be provided on the north side of the TVE to serve Llancaiach, Tophill and Gelligaer collieries.
3. Part of the Llancaiach branch, from the junction with the TVE line, was to be appropriated by the GWR for its station-to-station goods traffic in lieu of a siding then existing on the north side of the TVE line.
4. The TVR was to pay a toll for the use of the TVE line between Llancaiach and Quaker's Yard of 1½d. per ton on all coal and pitwood traffic hauled by TVR engines over this section from and to the Llancaiach collieries.

Under the provisions of this agreement, sidings were laid on the north side of the TVE line to serve Llancaiach, Tophill and Gelligaer collieries, thereby permitting the three level crossings to be removed. In addition, a junction was provided between the TVE and the Llancaiach branch, immediately to the west of Llancaiach station, which allowed the GWR to gain access to that part of the branch to be used for its goods traffic. On 3rd March, 1870 the TVR commenced working its coal and pitwood traffic from and to the Llancaiach collieries, via Quaker's Yard. Even though this involved increased mileage and a reversal at Quaker's Yard, traffic could be worked much more efficiently by this route than via the Llancaiach branch, with its rope-worked inclined plane. As a result, the Llancaiach branch fell into disuse, with the exception of the short section from Llancaiach Junction, used by the GWR. The junction with the TVR main line was taken out, as was a section of line on the adjoining inclined plane.

The original Llancaiach branch had lasted less than 30 years and had come to a premature end as a result of the inefficiencies inherent in its out-moded inclined plane. What appeared to be the final event in the story of this early branch came on 3rd February, 1871, when the TVR Board resolved to charge the cost (£1,420 11s. 10d.) of the new sidings to the collieries to the north of the TVE against revenue.

Chapter Three

The Taff Vale Railway Act 1873:
Background and Content

For the first 50 years of its life, the TVR, under the guidance of its energetic chief officer, George Fisher, pursued an expansionist policy of encouraging new sources of traffic through the promotion of or support for speculative or competitive lines. Fisher kept a constant eye on developments within or bordering the TVR's sphere of influence, including new opportunities and potential threats, and regularly presented his conclusions to his Directors in comprehensive and revealing reports.

In the early 1870s traffic on the TVR, especially coal from the Rhondda Valleys, was growing rapidly. There were a number of undeveloped areas capable of being served by the TVR, which, it was thought, could produce results comparable with those of the Rhondda Valleys. In the light of this consideration, George Fisher was asked to carry out surveys and report on possible lines to tap a number of potential sources of traffic, including the alteration of the disused Llancaiach branch, to make it suitable for locomotive haulage throughout its length, and a branch up the Clydach Valley, from the TVR main line. Fisher presented the results of his investigations to his Directors on 24th October, 1872. In the case of the Llancaiach branch, he noted that the object was to gain access to the undeveloped minerals of the Bargoed Taff Valley and the pits and works of the Dowlais Iron Co., together with the creation of a shorter route for coal and coke traffic from the Rhondda Valleys, destined for the Midland Counties and Birkenhead, via the TVE line and Pontypool Road. The attraction of the Clydach Valley, on the other hand, was the prospect of the opening up of undeveloped bituminous and steam coal reserves.

Having considered Fisher's report, the Directors gave instructions for the necessary detailed surveys to be carried out with a view to depositing plans and publishing notices for a Bill in the ensuing Session of Parliament.

The Bargoed Taff Valley

Penetration of the Bargoed Taff Valley had been an ambition of the TVR in its early days, but it was left to other companies to pursue this objective in later years. The valley itself was steeply graded and remote, but this was of little moment where there was coal to be worked. Its main attraction, however, was as a route to Dowlais, with its ironworks and associated coal pits. The works were connected to the TVR, at Merthyr, by the Dowlais Railway, with its rope-worked inclined plane, but by the late 1860s Dowlais had become a focus of attention for a number of railways, including the Brecon and Merthyr Railway (B&MR) and the LNWR.

Iron production in South Wales peaked in 1871 and from then on the picture was one of remorseless decline. The exception to this general trend, however, was the Dowlais Works, where technological innovation had always been a strong feature. In particular, Dowlais had introduced the new process for making mild steel, developed by Henry Bessemer, with the first, albeit limited, quantities appearing in 1865. As a result of this development, Dowlais continued to prosper where other works failed. The new process was unsuitable for use with the local ironstone, thereby necessitating the importation of high grade ore. For this what was needed was good direct access from the ports, something not provided by the existing railway facilities. Such an access was possible via the Bargoed Taff Valley, however, and, over the years, various attempts were made to promote a railway, via this route, to Dowlais. In addition to the ironworks, the Dowlais Iron Co. also owned a number of coal pits in the vicinity of Dowlais, connected to the works by a network of private railways across lonely and desolate moorland. The various schemes that emerged all sought to make use of such lines to secure the last section of the route into Dowlais.

Under the NA&HR (Branches) Act 1857 powers were obtained for the construction of a railway from the TVE, west of Llancaiach station, to a junction with the Dowlais Iron Co.'s railway, near Fochriw. However, in 1862 the West Midlands Railway (WMR), which had absorbed the NA&HR in July 1860, was authorised, under its Additional Works Act, to abandon this line. But this was not the end of the matter for in the following year the WMR sought and obtained fresh powers for a line up the Bargoed Taff Valley, on a new alignment and featuring, somewhat strangely, a junction with the Dowlais Iron Co.'s railway which faced away from Dowlais. Whilst the Bill was before Parliament, the WMR gave an undertaking to grant running powers to the TVR, over the proposed railway. In August 1863 the WMR became part of the GWR, which in its Further Powers Bill in the 1866 Session sought, unsuccessfully, to substitute a new route for the Bargoed Taff branch in place of the authorised WMR line, with a junction with the Dowlais Iron Co.'s railway which provided a direct run into Dowlais.

In November 1866 the GWR returned to the fray with fresh plans for a Bargoed Taff branch, as part of its Various Powers Bill for the 1867 Session. At the same time, the RR deposited plans for a railway from the B&MR, near Fochriw, in the Bargoed Rhymney Valley, to Dowlais. The RR made an end-on junction with the B&MR at Deri, lower down the valley and possessed running powers from there to Fochriw. In addition, a connecting line was proposed between the RR main line at Ystrad Mynach and the TVE line at Penallta.

Conflict between the two companies was averted, however, as a result of a meeting between their senior officers early in 1867, at which a compromise was agreed. This involved the pooling of the two schemes to produce a single proposal for a joint railway from Llancaiach to Dowlais. This was authorised under the GWR (Various Powers) Act, which received Royal Assent on 15th July, 1867. In addition to confirming the TVR's running powers between Llancaiach and Quaker's Yard, the Act also included similar powers in respect of the newly authorised railways. The RR Act of 12th August, 1867 confined itself to the authorisation of the Penallta branch, together with running powers to the company over the GWR between Hengoed and Hirwaun, thereby providing the RR with a direct access to the Aberdare Valley, in competition with the TVR.

The Taff Bargoed Joint Railway (TBJR) left the TVE line at Taff Bargoed Junction, to the west of Llancaiach station. This junction, together with its new signal box, was reported on favourably by Colonel Rich of the Board of Trade on 20th December, 1875. The Colonel returned to inspect the completed railway early in 1876, his report being dated 6th January. The line was opened to goods and mineral traffic on 10th January, 1876, and to passengers on 1st February of that year.

The Clydach Valley

A branch up the Clydach Valley had featured in the TVR's Bill in the 'Mania' Session of 1846. On 16th September, 1845 the company's Superintendent, Mr Highton, had been instructed to make a survey of the valley and in the following November plans were deposited for a branch from the TVR main line, at Glyncoch, to a waterfall, called 'Pistyll-goleu', near Llanwonno. The Clydach Valley was steeply graded throughout its length and the 1846 scheme differed markedly in its approach to this problem compared with the branch as later built. In a report to his Directors, dated 5th January, 1846, Highton noted that the proposed line was 'to be worked partly by self-acting inclines, partly by stationary engine and partly by locomotive engines', with an estimated cost of £59,204 11s. 3d. The TVR Board was clearly not impressed with this prospect and accordingly abandoned this part of the Bill.

A further attempt to promote a branch up the Clydach Valley came in 1862. On 29th October of that year the TVR Board was informed that Alexander Bassett, CE had applied to the company for pecuniary assistance in connection with an application to Parliament for powers to build such a branch. Bassett (1824-1887) was, at this time, Engineer to the ill-starred Cowbridge Railway Co. (incorporated on 29th July, 1862), but was also engaged, at this stage in his career, in the promotion of, or opposition to, various railway schemes in South Wales. He later became President of the South Wales Institute of Engineers. Having considered Bassett's approach, the TVR Directors agreed to inform him that when he was able to bring forward a scheme promoted by the landowners, the Board would give it full consideration. This may be the scheme referred to by George Fisher, in his report of 24th October, 1872, in which he noted that plans had been prepared for a Clydach Valley branch, some time before, 'by an independent party', but that the TVR Board had been of the opinion that the time had not then arrived for making the line and that the plans themselves were imperfect.

In 1872 the prospects for coal mining in the valley appeared encouraging. Traffic from the nearby Rhondda Valleys continued to grow apace, and there seemed good reason to expect a similar state of affairs in the Clydach Valley.

The 1873 Act

The plans deposited by the TVR in November 1872 included the following railways:

Railway No. 1:   a deviation line to avoid the old inclined plane and sharp curve on the disused Llancaiach branch.

Railway No. 2:   a junction between the Llancaiach branch and the TVE line, at Llancaiach. (This already existed, but the powers sought would confirm the TVR's rights.)

Railway No. 3:   an additional junction with the TVE line a short distance to the west of the junction of Railway No. 2. (This was close to the authorised junction of the TBJR, which itself was moved eastwards under an agreement between the GWR and the RR, dated 5th November, 1874.)

Railway No. 4:   an east curve at Llancaiach to join the TVE line, east of Llancaiach station.

Railway No. 5:   the Clydach Valley or Ynysybwl branch.

Railway No. 6:   a south curve between Railway No. 5 and the TVR main line, at Glyncoch.

In addition, running powers were sought over the TVE line from the junctions of the proposed Railways Nos. 2 and 3 to the junction with the authorised TBJR, running powers over the joint lines themselves having been obtained under the GWR (Various Powers) Act 1867.

Despite opposition from the GWR, all the proposed railways, with the exception of Railway No. 3, were authorised by the TVR Act of 21st July, 1873.* Three years were allowed for the compulsory purchase of lands and five years for the completion of works.   The Act also provided for the formal abandonment of the old inclined plane and sharp curve, near Fidler's Elbow, on the original Llancaiach branch.   The TVR was granted running powers, as requested, over the TVE as far as the authorised junction with the TBJR. However, the Act limited the use of Llancaiach Junction (as it became known) to the conveyance of traffic to and from the junction with the TBJR (Railway No. 1 of the GWR (Various Powers) Act 1867) together with that to and from the colliery sidings to the north of the TVR, at Llancaiach, and Harris's Navigation Colliery, at Treharris. With these running powers, coupled with those obtained under the GWR (Various Powers) Act 1867, the TVR believed it had secured a viable route to Harris's Navigation Colliery, the Bargoed Taff Valley and Dowlais.

---

* As the TVR Act 1873 did not include powers for the construction of intended Railway No. 3, the remaining lines (i.e. Railways Nos. 4 to 6) were renumbered in the Act, becoming Railways Nos. 3 to 5.

Chapter Four

The Llancaiach and
Pont Shon Norton Branches 1873-1900

The Llancaiach New Branch

Of the two main elements of the TVR Act of 1873, that involving the improvement of the old Llancaiach branch appears to have had the higher priority. In September 1875, just over two years after the passing of the Act, instructions were given to start work on the 'Llancaiach New Branch Railway', as it was referred to at the time. The new works proceeded without incident, the principal feature being the construction of a locomotive incline at a lower level than, but parallel to, the old inclined plane. By June 1878 the alterations were sufficiently complete for Board of Trade sanction to be sought for the new junction with the TVR main line. This junction, referred to as 'Stormstown Junction' in place of the old 'Llancaiach Branch Junction', was reported on by Colonel Rich of the Board of Trade on 26th June, 1878. Trailing connections only were provided to the up and down lines, with two loop sidings on the branch itself, the junction being controlled by a new signal cabin. Having reported the successful outcome of this inspection to his Directors on 4th July, 1878, George Fisher was asked to establish the probable date at which the branch itself would be ready for such inspection. Fisher duly reported, on 18th July, 1878, that the new line was ready for traffic, but that the points and signalling at the junction with the GWR at Llancaiach had not been completed.

The Act of 1873 also provided for an east curve between the TVR and the GWR, at Llancaiach. The formation of this curve was complete by March 1878, together with 24 chains of permanent way to the point of intended junction with the GWR. The junction itself was not formed as it was agreed between the two companies to refrain from installing it until it had been seen whether or not it could be justified by the likely traffic. On 24th July, 1878 the GWR gave an undertaking to lay the junction in question at any time, when required by the TVR, whether or not Parliamentary powers remained in force. Most of the curve was lifted in 1883, leaving only 7 chains in place, at the TVR end. This remnant was still there in 1898, but is believed to have been removed in connection with the upgrading of the Llancaiach branch for passenger use.

The western junction was sufficiently complete, on 1st August 1878, for the TVR Board to resolve to serve notice on the Bargoed Railways Joint Committee of intention to exercise its running powers as from 1st September, 1878. By this date, George Fisher's earlier enthusiasm for the use of the Llancaiach branch as a route to Dowlais had waned somewhat. In a report to his Directors, dated 15th August, 1878, he advised against such an approach, recommending instead that the company offer reduced rates for iron and other traffic, via the TVR main line and the Dowlais Railway. For Fisher, the main objective to be pursued, via the Llancaiach branch, was coal traffic from Harris's Navigation Colliery, near Treharris, and from the Bargoed Taff Valley itself.

Following the serving of this notice on the Joint Committee, a dispute arose

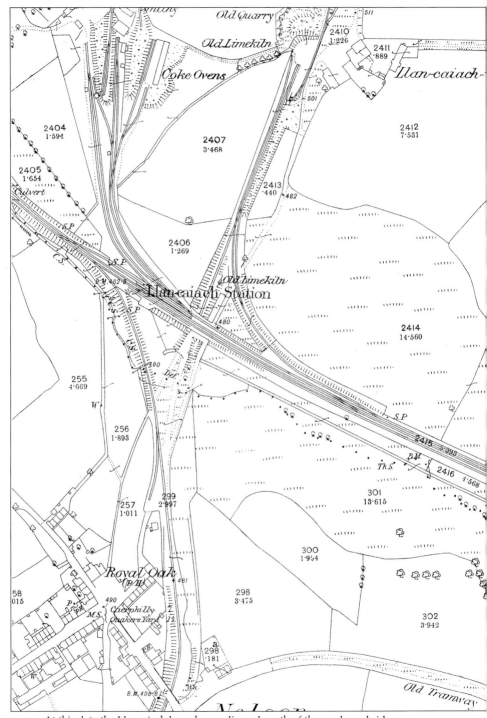

At this date the Llancaiach branch was disused south of the road overbridge.
Reproduced from 25″, 1873 Ordnance Survey Map

between the TVR and the GWR over the interpretation of the running powers granted by the GWR (Various Powers) Act 1867 and the TVR Act 1873. This issue remained unresolved and prevented use being made of the Llancaiach branch for through coal and other traffic from the GWR and TBJR lines, to the north of Llancaiach Junction, while the lines remained in separate ownership. Although the TVR had been granted running powers between Llancaiach and Quaker's Yard and between Llancaiach and Dowlais, the TVR Act of 1873 had stipulated that the junction between the Llancaiach branch and the GWR was only to be used for the purpose of conveying traffic to and from Harris's Navigation Colliery, the collieries north of the GWR at Llancaiach, and Taff Bargoed Junction with the TBJR. The GWR contended that the TVR was entitled only to exercise running powers from Llancaiach Junction as far as Taff Bargoed Junction, in order to make use of its running powers over the TBJR and disputed the TVR's view that it was entitled to work through to Harris's Navigation Colliery. As a result, no traffic passed over the Llancaiach branch and the TVR continued to haul its Llancaiach coal traffic via Quaker's Yard. On 5th May, 1880, following a meeting with James Hurman, the TVR's Traffic Manager, James Grierson, General Manager of the GWR, agreed to recommend to his Directors that the TVR be permitted to work to and from Harris's Navigation Colliery, via Llancaiach Junction, on the understanding that agreement was reached on the terms for the use of the GWR line for this purpose. Unfortunately, this did not lead to a formal agreement and so the impasse continued.

No further progress was made with this question until 1889. In October of that year the TVR issued fresh notices of intention to exercise its running powers from Llancaiach Junction, over the TBJR, in accordance with the provisions of the Acts of 1867 and 1873. This notice was not acted upon, however, and it subsequently emerged that the TVR had in mind a rather specific and limited application of the powers in question. The Dowlais Iron Co. had commenced sinking two pits at Aberdare Junction, and the TVR wished to convey stores and materials from Dowlais to the new sinkings, together with small coal in the reverse direction, via Llancaiach Junction. With these intentions clarified, Henry Lambert, GWR General Manager since the death of Grierson in 1887, suggested, by way of compromise, that the Joint Committee be responsible for working the traffic between Dowlais and Llancaiach Junction, for exchange with the TVR. This was agreed and operations over the Llancaiach branch commenced in the first week of November 1889, its first regular use for 19 years.

The Dowlais Iron Co.'s pits at Aberdare Junction were intended to reach the steam coal measures already proved by the Albion Colliery Co., at nearby Cilfynydd. On 5th December, 1889 the TVR Engineer was instructed to obtain tenders for the construction of a branch railway to serve these new pits, together with a bridge over the River Taff. Tenders were sought for these works and on 27th March, 1890 those of Johnson Brothers, in the case of the new railway, and Handyside & Co., for the river bridge, were accepted. The siding left the Llancaiach branch just above Stormstown Junction, but the colliery itself took some time to produce coal, and it was not until the middle of 1895 that the sought after seams were reached. The scale of this undertaking, to be known as the Dowlais-Cardiff Colliery, is indicated by its siding capacity, which in 1895 amounted to 424 wagons.

The TVR was less successful in its attempt to serve Harris's Navigation Colliery. Meetings took place between officers of the company and the GWR in February and June 1890, but a draft agreement was not completed. However, agreement was reached in 1890 whereby some coal traffic was brought to the Llancaiach branch. At a meeting with Henry Lambert and the GWR Solicitor on 14th February, 1890, James Hurman stated that the TVR wished to convey its coal from the Llancaiach collieries via the Llancaiach branch rather than via Quaker's Yard. For this privilege Hurman was prepared to pay ½d. per ton. Lambert, in response, asked for ¾d. but the two sides eventually settled at ⅝d. per ton. As a result, the TVR ceased to work over the GWR between Llancaiach and Quaker's Yard. Unfortunately, the traffic gained by the Llancaiach branch was but small reward for the expense incurred in upgrading the line. Llancaiach Colliery, which had been taken over by Powell's Gelligaer Colliery Co. in 1876, had closed in May 1881. That same year its proprietor, Walter Powell, had been lost in a balloon over the English Channel, presumed drowned. Powell's other colliery, at Gelligaer, had also closed in 1881, but was reactivated in the late 1880s. In 1891 it was being worked by one Edward Beddoe. Beddoe, together with a Mr James of Nelson, was also working a new, but confusingly titled 'Llancaiach Colliery' alongside the Gelligaer mine. Both had closed by 1907. Tophill Colliery, which had remained in the ownership of the Cartwright family, was finally closed in 1900. A single daily working over the branch sufficed for the traffic on offer, while it lasted.

The Pont Shon Norton Branch

The competitive environment faced by railways in South Wales in the 19th century was such that any unexploited opportunity or gap in defensive arrangements could quickly become a focus of attention for opponents, and others, who stood to profit from such situations. Between Pontypridd and Aberdare Junction the TVR main line stuck closely to the western side of the Taff Valley. The eastern side of the valley offered that rare commodity in the South Wales valleys - undeveloped space - together with the potential for conversion to railway use of the gradually decaying Glamorganshire Canal. As a result, it was always vulnerable to encroachment by competitors eager to break through to Merthyr and the Aberdare Valley. As early as 1865, plans had been deposited for a railway from Mountain Ash to join the RR main line, near Caerphilly, passing down the eastern side of the Taff Valley, *en route*. This scheme, the Aberdare Valley and Caerphilly Junction Railway (AV&CJR), was the brainchild of George Elliot, Manager of the Powell Duffryn Steam Coal Co., which owned a number of collieries in the Aberdare Valley, and colliery owner John Nixon. Although the AV&CJR failed to reach the statute book, the Rhymney Railway later achieved access to the lucrative traffic of the Aberdare Valley by means of its Penallta branch from Ystrad Mynach and the grant of running powers over the GWR between Penallta Junction and Hirwaun under its Act of 12th August, 1867. Nevertheless, the undeveloped eastern side of the Taff Valley, between Aberdare Junction and Pontypridd continued to present an enticing prospect for companies and promoters wishing to get to the Aberdare Valley.

In November 1877 a notice was published of an intended Bill for the Pontypridd Caerphilly and Newport Railway (PC&NR), which included a branch from the proposed 'main line', near Glyntaff, to Pont Shon Norton, about a mile north of Pontypridd, on the eastern side of the Taff Valley. This particular feature did not survive to appear in the Bill, as printed, but must have set alarm bells ringing at the TVR headquarters in Crockherbtown, Cardiff, especially as a leading promoter of the PC&NR was George Elliot, by then Managing Director of the Powell Duffryn Co.

The PC&NR Act received Royal Assent on 8th August, 1878, and authorised the construction of a railway from Pontypridd to Caerphilly (Railway No. 1), together with a line bypassing the section of the RR through Caerphilly (Railway No. 2), which was subsequently abandoned. The threat of a northward extension of the PC&NR was no doubt fresh in the minds of the TVR Directors when, on 18th July, 1878, they requested George Fisher to examine the question of a loop line along the eastern side of the Taff Valley from a point above Pontypridd to a junction with the Llancaiach New Branch Railway. Writing in December 1878, George Fisher stated that the object of this line was to accommodate certain properties where there were believed to be large quantities of steam coal; indeed one such property had already been let for that purpose and the lessees were actively sinking for coal. However, given the context of this proposal, it must also be seen as a defensive move on the part of the TVR to protect an exposed and vulnerable flank. Fisher placed the plans of the requested line before his Directors on 17th October, 1878 and was instructed to prepare notices and plans for the ensuing Parliamentary Session. Earlier that month, Fisher's opposite number at the RR, Cornelius Lundie, had received similar instructions concerning an extension from the authorised PC&NR, near Glyntaff, along the eastern side of the Taff Valley to Navigation House. There the line was to divide, with one arm going to Nixon's Navigation Colliery, at Mountain Ash, in the Aberdare Valley, and the other, following the line of the by then defunct Merthyr Tramroad, to the same company's Merthyr Vale Colliery. At this time the RR was actively negotiating with the TVR with a view to merging with the larger company, and it appears that the proposed railways were intended to put pressure on the TVR to secure an outcome more favourable to the Rhymney Co.'s interests.

The plans deposited by the TVR in November 1878 comprised two short railways: one from a junction with the TVR main line, just over ½ mile north of Pontypridd, to Cilfynydd Inn, on the eastern side of the Taff Valley, mid-way between Pontypridd and Stormstown Junction, and the other from an end-on junction with this line at Cilfynydd Inn to a point near to the Llancaiach branch, just beyond its bridge over the Glamorganshire Canal. One intriguing feature is that although the Notice of the Bill makes it clear that the second railway would terminate on TVR land, the Deposited Plans clearly show that the line

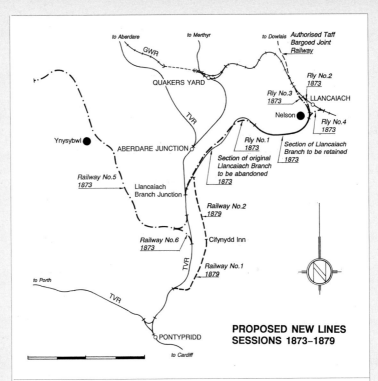

PROPOSED NEW LINES
SESSIONS 1873–1879

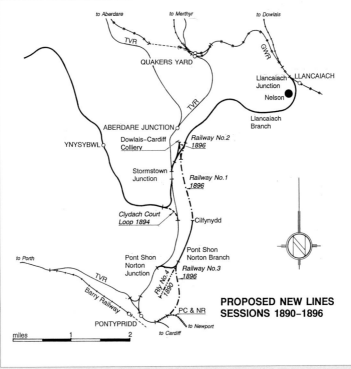

PROPOSED NEW LINES
SESSIONS 1890–1896

was to stop short of an actual junction with the Llancaiach branch.

The RR Bill was withdrawn after its first reading, leaving only the line from the TVR main line to Cilfynydd Inn to be authorised by that company's Act of 21st July, 1879. Negotiations for the amalgamation of the RR with the TVR came to an abrupt halt in 1882, when the former company renewed its attempt to expand further into TVR territory, this time in the form of a railway from the GWR, at Quaker's Yard, to Merthyr. The GWR also proposed a similar line and, in a re-run of the Taff Bargoed settlement of 1867, it was agreed to pool the two schemes to produce a joint line, this being authorised by the RR Act of 18th August, 1882.

Whatever the motive behind the promotion of the Pont Shon Norton branch (as it became known), whether defensive or speculative, the TVR displayed a distinct lack of urgency in building the authorised line. An extension of time for the completion of the railway was obtained under the TVR Act of 12th July, 1882, but the company still showed no great inclination to start work. However, the situation changed markedly in November 1882, when the PC&NR deposited plans for its long-threatened extension into the Aberdare Valley. The proposed line was to leave the main line of the PC&NR, then under construction, at a point near Glyntaff, and was to pass up the eastern side of the Taff Valley and into the Aberdare Valley, where it was to make use of the private railway, then being built by John Nixon, and the Powell Duffryn Railway to reach the Aman Valley. In the event, Parliament was not convinced that such a line would serve the public interest, and this part of the Bill was thrown out on the grounds that its preamble was not proven.

This further threat to territory it regarded as its own appears to have had a salutary effect on the TVR, for on 13th September, 1883, John Williams, the company's engineer responsible for new works, was instructed to purchase the land required for the Pont Shon Norton branch. Doubtless, the company was also influenced by reports that coal speculator Ebenezer Lewis of Newport was about to sink a new colliery at Ynyscaedwdwg Farm, near Cilfynydd Inn. The Albion Steam Coal Co. was formed to develop the colliery and in December 1884 sinking for coal began in earnest, the first marketable coal being raised in August 1887. The colliery was the scene of a major disaster on 23rd June, 1894, when an underground explosion resulted in the deaths of 290 men and boys.

On 7th January, 1884 the *Western Mail* reported that work was about to start on the new railway, and on 23rd April of that year the TVR applied for Board of Trade sanction for a siding connection to the works on the new line. This was reported on by Colonel Rich on 16th May, 1884 and comprised a trailing connection to the down main line, with a trailing crossover between the running lines on the main line. The whole was under the control of a new signal box, bearing the name Pont Shon Norton Junction.

A short branch southwards from the Pont Shon Norton branch was authorised by the TVR Act of 25th July, 1890, with the intention of serving a proposed colliery, near Coedpenmaen. This colliery was not proceeded with, however, but the powers for the construction of the branch railway were kept alive by extensions of time in successive Acts, the last of which received Royal Assent in 1912.

The viaduct over the River Taff on the Pont Shon Norton branch, possibly at the time of its completion in 1885. *Welsh Industrial & Maritime Museum*

The Cilfynydd Loop under construction alongside Albion Colliery, Cilfynydd, *c.* 1898.
Welsh Industrial & Maritime Museum

Completion of the Network

In the 1890s south-east Wales was the scene of frenzied competition between the various local railway companies, and, for a time, the eastern side of the Taff Valley, between Pontypridd and Aberdare Junction, became an intense battlefield for rival schemes. Undoubtedly, the most aggressive local company was the Barry Railway (ByR) and in October 1893 it agreed to support a nominally independent concern, the East Glamorgan Railway (EGR), in its application to Parliament. The EGR was clearly a creature of the Barry Co.: eight of its nine Directors were also members of the Barry Board. It was intended to tap the upper part of the Rhymney Valley, together with Bargoed Taff Valley, and followed unsuccessful attempts by the Barry Co. to reach the RR in 1889 (via Llanishen) and 1891 (via Penrhos Junction). The plans for the EGR, deposited in November 1893, involved a line from the ByR main line, near Pontypridd, passing close to Pont Shon Norton, before taking a higher level route to Nelson, where the line was to divide, one arm going off to join the Taff Bargoed Joint Railway, while the other continued to Bargoed, where junctions were to be made with the RR and the B&MR. The EGR Bill met with considerable opposition on the part of the TVR and the RR and was thrown out by the Committee of the House of Lords. The Barry Co. returned undaunted in the following Session with a similar scheme, this time without the pretence of independence, but this too was rejected. Having thus been twice rebuffed, the ByR revived its earlier scheme to reach the RR, by way of Penrhos. This proved more successful and the railway from Tynycaeau Junction on the Barry's main

Pontypridd Junction *c.* 1890. This scene gives a good indication of the congested conditions that existed prior to the rebuilding of the station. *Author's Collection*

The connection from the Cilfynydd Loop to Dowlais-Cardiff Colliery under construction, with the bridge carrying the Nelson branch from Stormstown Junction nearing completion, *c.* 1899.
Welsh Industrial & Maritime Museum

A bridge carrying the Cilfynydd Loop over a stream at Cilfynydd nearing completion in 1899.
Welsh Industrial & Maritime Museum

line to Penrhos Junction on the RR was authorised by the ByR Act of 7th August, 1896, and was opened to goods and mineral traffic on 1st August, 1901. The attempt to reach the Bargoed Taff Valley was not given up entirely, however, for in the 1896 Session a Bill was introduced for the 'Taff and Bargoed Junction Railway', from the Llancaiach branch to join the TBJR. This proposal had the backing of certain Barry Directors, but was withdrawn in April 1896.

The 1896 Session of Parliament witnessed the peak of competitive activity in the area between Pontypridd and Abercynon (as Aberdare Junction was known by the TVR from this date). The TVR sought to underline its dominance in the area by seeking powers for three new railways:

Railway No. 1:   an extension of the Pont Shon Norton branch to join the Llancaiach branch, above Stormstown Junction (this line was usually known as the 'Clifynydd Loop').

Railway No. 2:   a branch from Railway No. 1 to the Dowlais Iron Co.'s Dowlais-Cardiff Colliery.

Railway No. 3:   a loop line from the Pont Shon Norton branch to join the PC&NR, near Glyntaff.

Running powers were sought over the section of the PC&NR between the junction of proposed Railway No. 3 and PC&N Junction, at Pontypridd. It was intended that passenger trains would be introduced between Nelson and Pontypridd, routed via Railway No. 3 to avoid the congested northern approaches to Pontypridd station. Railways Nos. 1 and 2 would provide an alternative route for coal from the Dowlais-Cardiff Colliery, at Abercynon, then starting to produce in quantity. Taken as a whole, however, the proposed lines would knit together the various branches on the eastern side of the Taff Valley to produce a coherent network, with which the TVR would be better able to resist the threat of incursion by competitive lines. Proof of the strategic importance of the proposed railways can be gained from the report of the Chairman to the half-yearly meeting of TVR shareholders on 4th February, 1896, in which he stated, in reference to the Cilfynydd Loop, that 'This line, although short, is of considerable importance to the company, and if proof of that fact were needed it would be found in the endeavours of the Bute and Rhymney Companies to get powers for constructing a line along the same route'.

The RR Co.'s proposal involved a renewal of its earlier attempt to obtain powers for a northward extension from the PC&NR, although this time only as far as the Dowlais-Cardiff Colliery and a junction nearby with the Llancaiach branch. Far more spectacular was the Bute Docks Co.'s scheme for no less than 19 railways between Cardiff and Merthyr, Aberdare and Dowlais, making use of the bed of the Glamorganshire Canal for much of its length, including the section between Pontypridd and Abercynon. This grandiose proposal was withdrawn early in 1896, leaving Parliament to adjudicate between the merits of the TVR and RR Bills. The RR Bill fell foul of the Committee of the House of Lords, which found its preamble not proven, leaving the TVR lines to be authorised by the company's Act of 7th August, 1896. In the event, Railway No. 3 was not built, although powers for its construction were kept alive through to

1917 and land was acquired for much of its route.

In 1897 the Bute Docks Co. obtained powers for railways from the RR main line, at Heath, to a junction with the TVR, at Treforest, with a branch from Glyntaff to Coedpenmaen, which was not proceeded with, together with a change of name to the 'Cardiff Railway'. Not content with this relatively modest authorisation, the company returned to Parliament in the 1898 Session with a reworking of its mammoth scheme of 1896, only to see most of its proposals rejected, following strenuous opposition from the TVR and the RR. In the same Session the TVR sought, unsuccessfully, to gain unhindered running powers from the Llancaiach branch over the TBJR. After this hectic period, attention shifted to other parts of the South Wales Coalfield and no further attempt was made to break the TVR's monopoly of the ground between Pontypridd and Abercynon.

Following the passing of the TVR Act of 1896, discussions took place between representatives of the TVR and the GWR with a view to providing a joint station for the two companies at Llancaiach. Unfortunately, these failed to bear fruit, and the TVR proceeded on the basis that it would provide its own passenger facilities at Nelson.

At this date, Pont Shon Norton Junction remained very much in the form in which it had been installed in 1884, with a trailing connection to the down main line and trailing crossover only. For the introduction of a passenger service a double junction was required between the main line and the Pont Shon Norton branch. Although the Cilfynydd Loop was intended to provide relief for traffic from the Dowlais-Cardiff Colliery, it could do little to relieve conditions on the busy main line between Abercynon and Pontypridd. A down relief line was proposed, therefore, between Pont Shon Norton Junction and Pontypridd Northern Junction. Such a line had been authorised in 1889, but had not been proceeded with. On 5th October, 1898 the Traffic Committee approved various improvements at Pont Shon Norton Junction, at an estimated cost of £5,050. In addition to the new double junction, a connection was laid in from the Pont Shon Norton branch to the new down relief line, just beyond the junction. A new signal cabin was erected, containing 55 levers, of which 44 were in use. At Pontypridd Northern Junction the relief line joined a shunting siding provided in 1888 in connection with the opening of the new goods station at Pontypridd. The alterations at Pont Shon Norton Junction were reported on favourably by Colonel Yorke for the Board of Trade on 31st July, 1899. The junction in its unaltered form, had been the scene of a derailment involving a Merthyr-Cardiff passenger train, hauled by a class 'C' 4-4-2T No. 171, on 10th April, 1894.

The contractors appointed for the construction of the new railways between Cilfynydd and the Llancaiach branch and Dowlais-Cardiff Colliery were John Aird & Co. Operations proceeded without incident, the most significant engineering work being a bridge under the Llancaiach branch on the short spur to Dowlais-Cardiff Colliery. On 30th May, 1899 the Traffic Committee approved expenditure on three stations on the new line:

Norton Bridge (Coedpenmaen)	£1,074
Cilfynydd	£1,266
Nelson	£950

Work on the new lines was completed early in 1900 and on 2nd April of that year application was made for Board of Trade sanction for the introduction of passenger trains. On 25th May, 1900 Colonel Yorke inspected the new works, together with the earlier sections of line which had not previously been inspected. His report stated:

These lines may be conveniently divided into four 'works' or sections:

Work No. 1: Pont Shon Norton branch authorised in 1879 and in use for mineral traffic since 1885. This line commences at the Pont Shon Norton Junction with the main line of the Taff Vale Railway north of Pontypridd and terminates at Cilfynydd Loop junction with Work No. 2.

The total length of this line is 1 mile 10½ chains; it is single throughout and the gauge is 4 ft 8½ in. Sufficient land has been taken for a double line, but the works are constructed for a single line.

The permanent was is of Taff Vale standard pattern; viz, bullhead steel 30 ft rails 82 lb. per yard; chairs 42 lb. each and sleepers 9 ft by 10 in. by 5 in. The chairs are secured to the sleepers by three fang bolts. The bottom ballast is of stone and the top ballast of stone and ashes.

The steepest gradient is 1 in 183 and the sharpest curve has a radius of 12 chains.

The principal cutting is 25 ft deep and the highest embankment has a height of 21 ft.

There are three bridges under the line, one having a stone arch, one having steel girders (15 ft span) and one (25 ft span) having wrought iron girders. There is also a viaduct of 3 spans (the largest having a square opening of 67 ft or 80 ft on skew) consisting of wrought iron lattice girders with piers and abutments of stone masonry. There are also two culverts 5 ft or 6 ft in diameter.

All these works appear to be substantially built and to be standing well, and the girders under the line give moderate deflections under test. The line is fenced for the greater part of its length with post and rail fencing.

There is one station, viz. Coedpenmaen, which consists of a single platform (there being no loop) with booking hall, waiting room, ladies room and conveniences for both sexes.

There are no signals on this line, except at its commencement at Pont Shon Norton Junction, the signalling at which was inspected and reported upon by me sometime ago. There are three siding connections on the line, viz. one at a traffic siding near Pont Shon Norton Junction and two at Taylor's Quarry Siding at 50 chains from the commencement of the line. Each of these connections is worked by a ground frame containing two levers which are locked by the key on the Electric Train Staff and is fitted with the usual facing point safety appliances.

The only requirements I noted are that the staging for the Ground Frame at the lower end of Taylor's Quarry Siding should be made larger, and that the safety catch points at either end should be altered so as to prevent any risk of the main line being fouled by wagons which might be derailed at these points.

Work No. 2: Railway No. 1 authorised in 1896. This line commences at the Ynysydwr Junction with the Llancaiach branch of the Taff Vale Railway and terminates at its junction with the Pont Shon Norton branch (Work No. 1) at Cilfynydd. The total length of this line is 1 mile 2 furlongs and 9 chains and it is single throughout.

The permanent way is similar to that already availed to on Work No. 1. The steepest gradient has an inclination of 1 in 40, end the sharpest curve a radius of 15 chains.

There is an embankment having a maximum height of 35 ft, but the cuttings are unimportant.

There is one overbridge and two underbridges in this work; one of the latter having a brick arch and one being built with steel girders on stone abutments. The overbridge has two openings which are constructed with steel girders on stone abutments and steel piers. These works are substantially built and seem to be standing up well and the girders under the line gave moderate deflections when tested.

There is one station on this line, viz. Cilfynydd, which consists of a single platform (there being no loop line or sidings) on which proper accommodation of the usual description is provided, including conveniences for both sexes. There are connections at Cilfynydd Signal Box (about 1 furlong from the Station of the same name) at the north end of Cilfynydd loop, and at Dowlais Pit Sidings.

Cilfynydd Signal Box contains 11 levers in use and 1 spare lever, and the interlocking is correct. This is a Staff station, and a passing place for two goods trains or for a passenger train and a goods train, but not two passenger trains.

The connection at the southern end of Cilfynydd loop* and at Dowlais Pit siding are each worked by a 2 lever ground frame, locked by the key on the Train Staff.

Work No. 3: This is Railway No. 1 of the Act 1873. It commences at Ynysydwr Junction with Work No. 2 and terminates by an end-on junction with the Llancaiach Branch authorised by the Company's Act of 1836 (Work No. 4). This line has been in service since 1878 for mineral traffic. Its length is 1 mile 30 chains and it is single throughout.

The permanent way is of the standard pattern of the TVR. The steepest gradient is 1 in 40 and the sharpest curve has a radius of 10 chains. The deepest cutting has depth of 61 ft and the highest embankment a height of 17 ft 6 in.

There are three bridges over and one under the line. The underbridge has wrought iron girders resting on stone abutments. All the works appear to be substantially built and the girders under the line gave moderate deflections when tested.

There are no stations on this work, and no sidings at Ynysydwr Junction. The signal box at Ynysydwr Junction contains 8 levers in use and 2 spare levers, and the interlocking is correct. This is a Staff station, but as there is no passing loop, but only a siding it may not be used as a passing place for two passenger trains, but only for two goods trains, or for a goods train and a passenger train.

Work No. 4: This forms a portion of the Llancaiach branch of the TVR which was authorised by Act of 1836, and has been in use for mineral traffic since 1841. It is 1 mile 2 furlongs 4 chains in length and is single throughout. The permanent way is of the Taff Vale standard pattern and is in good order. The steepest gradient is 1 in 200 and the sharpest curve has a radius of 17 chains. The principal cutting and embankments are respectfully [sic] in height and 23 ft in depth. There is one overbridge of wrought iron and one underbridge having three segmented arch openings. These works appear to be substantially built and to be standing well.

The Company intend to work the whole of these new passenger lines on the Electric Train Staff system and have already provided an undertaking to that effect.

As the permanent way is in good order and the other arrangements are satisfactory, I can recommend the Board of Trade to sanction the use of the line referred to in this report for passenger traffic.

With Board of Trade approval secured, the TVR was now able to proceed with the introduction of a passenger train service between Pontypridd and Nelson.

---

* Colonel Yorke appears to be confused concerning north and south: Cilfynydd signal box was at the southern end of the loop, with the ground frame at the northern end.

Chapter Five

The Ynysybwl Branch, 1873-1900

The Ynysybwl branch was very much in the speculative tradition, but without corresponding activity on the part of colliery developers and other entrepreneurs, there was no great incentive for its early completion. As a result, the TVR, in spite of having promoted the Act for its construction in 1873 with some enthusiasm, showed no great sense of urgency in commencing operations. In June 1874, frustrated by this lack of action, various landowners, lessees of minerals and inhabitants of the Clydach Valley presented a Memorial to the TVR urging the necessity for the speedy construction of the railway. Having been requested to report further on the matter, George Fisher suggested, at the meeting of the Board on 25th June, 1874, that enquiries should be made to establish whether or not landowners in the valley would be prepared to sell their land for a 'reasonable' price to enable the railway to be built more cheaply. He did not meet with much success with his approaches to landowners, however, and on 23rd July, 1874, the Board decided to serve them with the usual notices to treat in respect of the land which was to be acquired compulsorily. At the next meeting on 25th August, 1874, Fisher submitted an estimate of £4,125 for the cost of the land involved.

Little progress had been made beyond this, when, on 8th November, 1877, the TVR Directors agreed to seek an extension of time for the completion of the Ynysybwl branch. A certain lack of commitment was evident, however, as they also decided to abandon the south curve at Glyncoch, which had also been authorised under the Act of 1873. The necessary powers were granted under the TVR Act of 4th July, 1878, the time limit for the completion of the branch being extended by three years. However, this extension of time merely kept alive the statutory powers, and by January 1880 pressure for action had increased considerably. On 29th of that month, a further Memorial from parties interested in the valley was placed before the TVR Directors. In it great play was made of the onerous obligations that had been entered into by colliery proprietors and mineral lessees in anticipation of the construction of the authorised railway. Faced with these pressures, the TVR Directors relented and instructed George Fisher to proceed with work on the branch. Tenders were sought and that of J.E. Billups, a contractor responsible for much work on the TVR, was accepted on 14th October, 1880.

After the years of procrastination, a fairly rapid start was made on the actual construction; on 8th December, 1880 application was made to the Board of Trade for sanction for a siding connection at Stormstown Junction for use with the works on the branch. This was the subject of a favourable report by Colonel Rich on 23rd December, 1880, and comprised a trailing connection to the up main line, just south of the junction with the Llancaiach branch. In June 1881 the *Pontypridd Observer* noted that 'already a road whereon the outcome of the Stephensons' modest investion may be allowed to have its run' had made its appearance in the valley.

After such a promising start, the rate of progress proved somewhat lacklustre. The valley had not attracted colliery development as anticipated, and without such development there remained no great incentive for early completion of the railway. What mining activity there was consisted of a few small levels. In March and July 1884 the TVR accepted applications for ledger accounts from the Mynachdy and Black Grove colliery companies, respectively. The former was near the village of Ynysybwl, while the latter was further up the valley, although their siding connections with the branch were quite close to each other. Prospects improved dramatically later in 1884 with the formation of the consortium Davies, Scott & Co. to sink Lady Windsor Colliery, south of Ynysybwl. The colliery was named after the wife of the landowner, Lord Windsor, and the prime mover behind the project was David Davies ('Davies the Ocean'), the celebrated railway builder, colliery owner, benefactor and promoter of the Barry Dock and Railways. The colliery was sunk in 1885, with the first marketable coal being produced in December 1886. In 1887 Davies, Scott & Co. became part of the Ocean Steam Coal Co., the private siding agreement between this concern and the TVR being dated 13th July, 1887. Lady Windsor Colliery was a substantial undertaking by any standard, employing 891 men in 1890.

About half-way up the Clydach Valley was the small rural settlement of Ynysybwl, its English translation 'island in the pass', providing an appropriate description of its setting and character. As early as September 1881 a Memorial had been submitted from farmers and others of Ynysybwl and its neighbourhood seeking the provision of a goods siding to serve the village. On 11th March, 1886 the TVR Board accepted the tender of Dixon & Co. for the erection of a goods warehouse at Ynysybwl, for the sum of £49. This was opened by July 1886, but appears to have been removed or destroyed at a later date, possibly by 24th November, 1887, when a deputation attended the TVR Board on the subject of the warehouse. The siding at this place was subsequently known as 'Old Warehouse Siding'.

The opening of the goods warehouse at Ynysybwl brought with it the commencement of general goods traffic over the branch. However, it seems likely that other traffic was conveyed before this event. Materials were needed for use in developing new mines, and coal may have been moved from Mynachdy and Black Grove in 1885, or even 1884. Undoubtedly, the sinking of Lady Windsor Colliery in 1885 would have required the transport, by rail, of substantial quantities of stores and construction materials.

One unusual feature of the Ynysybwl branch, at its opening, was that unlike the rest of the TVR, and other independent lines in South Wales, where trains worked 'up' the valley and 'down' to the sea, here the reverse was the case, with branch trains working 'up' to Stormstown Junction. There was, of course, a logical explaination, as the junction at Stormstown took the form of a trailing connection into the up line to Merthyr. However, following the opening, in 1900, of the Clydach Court Loop, which provided a direct run from the branch towards Pontypridd, the normal arrangement was introduced, with trains running 'up' the line to Ynysybwl, and 'down' to Pontypridd.

The sinking of Lady Windsor Colliery in 1885 brought with it rapid development of new housing at Blackrock, about ½ mile below Ynysybwl village, and also further down the valley, nearer the colliery itself. Initially, the upper area was referred to as 'Blackrock' or 'Clivetown', but later it became known as Ynysybwl, leaving the original village to be known as 'Old Ynysybwl'. Such changes can cause much confusion to the historian! Robertstown was the name applied to the lower area, adjacent to Lady Windsor Colliery, but in this case the name did not fall out of use. Both Clivetown and Robertstown were named after the landowner, Robert George Windsor-Clive (1857-1923), otherwise Lord Windsor.

In the face of such rapid growth, the limited facilities on the branch soon proved inadequate for the needs of the traffic on offer. Pressure also grew for the introduction of a passenger train service. On 16th December, 1886 the TVR Traffic Manager, James Hurman, was requested to report on the need for additional accommodation at Ynysybwl. In his report, dated 6th January, 1887, Hurman pointed out that for several months traffic to and from Blackrock had been severely hampered by the lack of suitable facilities: there were only two short sidings available, capable of holding a total of only 12 wagons. On many occasions there had been 40 or more wagons standing at Stormstown Junction, waiting to be taken up the branch. Hurman's report contained some interesting details concerning the state of development in the valley. There were already 350 houses at Blackrock, with a further 75 under construction, the population being put at 1,423 persons. Further down the valley, nearer the colliery, there were 135 houses, with 25 more under construction and an estimated population of 334.

Prospects for further development were clearly encouraging and provided the background to correspondence which had taken place between TVR engineer for new works, John Williams, and Robert Forrest, agent to Lord Windsor. Forrest had formulated a proposal with a Mr Shepherd, a contractor engaged on building operations in the area, which he wished to put to the TVR. Under this proposal, Shepherd was to excavate a tunnel under the rock outcrop, which gave its name to the settlement, in order to divert the River Clydach. At this point the river took the form of a very tight loop, which was bridged at two points by the Ynysybwl branch. The railway was also crossed, on the level, by a road which gave access to Lady Windsor Colliery. The proposed river tunnel was intended to provide Shepherd with stone for building purposes, and, for this work, he sought a payment of £600, in return for which he was prepared to pay a low royalty of 2d. per ton on the rock so obtained. In exchange, the TVR would gain possession, free of charge, from Lord Windsor, of land, then occupied by the River Clydach and its banks, for the erection of a station. Additional benefits to the TVR included the removal of a dangerous level crossing and the avoidance of maintenance of two river bridges. Besides acquiring land for a station, the TVR would also gain a valuable frontage to the main road. For Lord Windsor a new station would clearly enhance the value of his property, besides making development itself easier.

Hurman's report was considered at the meeting of the Board on 6th January, 1887, but a decision was deferred so that the Directors could take the opportunity of seeing the ground for themselves. Evidently, they were

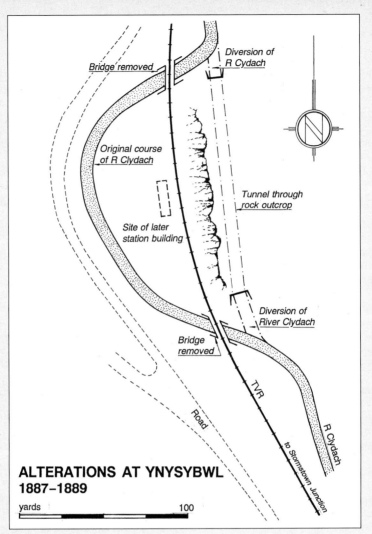

Bridge removed

Diversion of R Cydach

Original course of R Clydach

Tunnel through rock outcrop

Site of later station building

Diversion of River Clydach

Bridge removed

TVR

Road

R Clydach

to Stormstown Junction

ALTERATIONS AT YNYSYBWL
1887–1889

yards   100

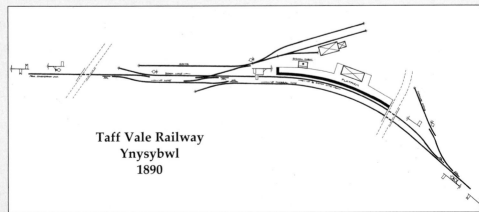

**Taff Vale Railway
Ynysybwl
1890**

favourably impressed with what they saw, as, on 9th June, 1887, instructions were given to the Engineer to prepare plans and an estimate for a station, goods warehouse and bridge over the railway. Later that month the Engineer was asked to prepare a detailed specification and to seek tenders for the works involved. On 28th July, 1887 the tender of Messrs Logan and Hemingway was accepted for the construction of the station and associated works, for the sum of £3,360 7s. 9d., subject to satisfactory arrangements being made with Lord Windsor for the possession of the necessary land. On 26th January, 1888 George Fisher was authorised to sign the contract with Logan & Hemingway for the erection of station building, warehouse and platform at Ynysybwl station. Construction of the new station was dependent upon the completion of the tunnel and the diversion of the River Clydach. The tunnel itself was 123 yards long and was unlined throughout its length. With the river diverted, the two redundant river bridges could be removed, the land levelled and the new facilities put in place. An overbridge was also constructed, immediately to the north of the new station, to carry the road to Lady Windsor Colliery.

In addition to the new station, other works were necessary in order to bring the line up to an appropriate standard for passenger use. In particular, the layout at Stormstown Junction needed to be changed from a simple siding connection to a fully signalled double junction. On 14th November, 1889 instructions were given for tenders to be obtained for this work, which was undertaken with sufficient speed to enable Board of Trade approval to be sought, on 25th November, 1889, for the introduction of a passenger train service over the line between Stormstown Junction and Ynysybwl station. Colonel Rich inspected the railway and his report, dated 21st December, 1889, stated:

> The new line is 2 miles 2½ chains long. It commences by a junction with the Taff Vale mineral line at Ynysybwl and ends at Stormstown Junction where it joins the Taff Vale line to Aberdare Junction. It is a single line with sidings. The land has been enclosed for a double line. The permanent way is of the Taff Vale standard pattern. It is in good order and the railway is well fenced. The ruling gradient is 1 in 40 and the sharpest curve has a radius of 14 chains.
>
> The Works consist of two overbridges that have stone abutments and wooden tops and one that has iron girders on stone abutments. One underbridge has wooden beams on stone abutments and there are three viaducts which carry the Railway over the mountain streams. Two of these consist of three openings and the third has two openings. They have stone abutments end piers and wooden tops. These works are all of sufficient strength.
>
> The junction cabin at Ynysybwl has 20 working and 5 spare levers. The junction cabin at Stormstown has 32 working and 8 spare levers.
>
> There are no stations on the new line.
>
> The following works are required. The runaway catch points at Ynysybwl should be self-acting. At Stormstown Junction No. 24 lever should be interlocked with No. 34.
>
> I enclose a satisfactory undertaking as to the proposed mode of working and can recommend the Board of Trade to sanction the opening of the new railway subject to the above mentioned alterations being made.

Strangely, the inspection report makes no mention of the passing loop and

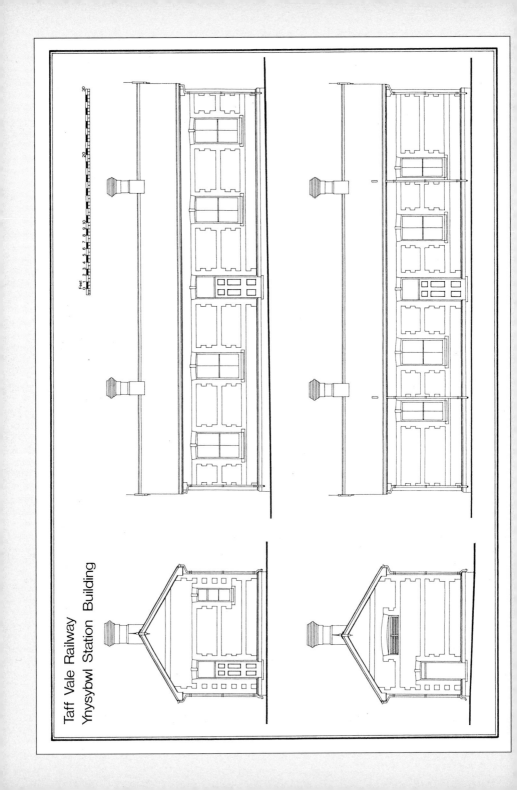

Taff Vale Railway
Ynysybwl Station Building

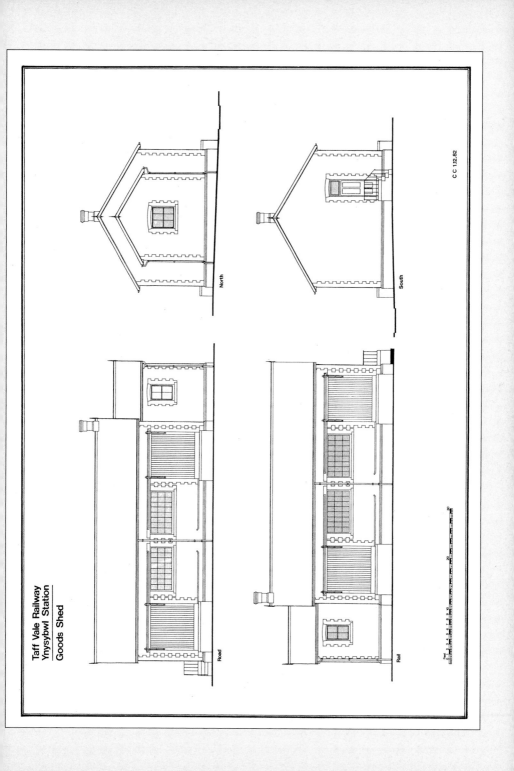

Taff Vale Railway
Ynysybwl Station
Goods Shed

North

South

Road

Rail

C C 1:12.82

signal box at Windsor Passing Siding, where the line from Lady Windsor Colliery joined the branch. However, the existence of both is confirmed in the TVR instructions for the opening for passenger traffic, issued on 30th December, 1889.

Board of Trade approval of the railway and new works enabled a passenger train service to be introduced between Aberdare Junction and Ynysybwl on Wednesday 1st January, 1890. The inaugural service, which comprised a very basic three trains each way, was not celebrated in any formal sense on the opening day. Instead, it was arranged that the opening should be commemorated on the following Monday, 6th January, 1890, when a procession was organised, made up of workmen, tradesmen and schoolchildren, and led by members of the Ynysybwl Choral Society. After the parade, a picnic tea was held for schoolchildren and Lady Windsor Colliery doorboys. It would clearly have been churlish, on such an occasion, to have complained about the sparse service provided by the TVR, but hopes were expressed that the traffic on the branch would soon justify the provision of something better.

In 1891 improvements were carried out at Stormstown Junction in conjunction with the installation of a down passing siding between that place and Aberdare Junction. A connection was put in from the Ynysybwl branch to new sidings on the up side of the main line, together with a trailing connection to these sidings from the down main line. The works concerned were carried out by J.E. Billups, whose tender had been accepted by the TVR on 8th January, 1891. They were notified as ready for inspection on 4th August, 1891, and were inspected by Colonel Rich, who completed his report to the Board of Trade on 10th August, 1891. These alterations considerably eased shunting operations at the junction for the growing coal traffic off the branch.

Use of Aberdare Junction by Ynysybwl passenger trains was unsatisfactory in a number of respects, not the least being the accommodation available there. On 25th October, 1892, Ammon Beasley, then recently appointed General Manager of the TVR, noted, in a memorandum to his Directors, that the facilities at Aberdare Junction would, in all probability, soon be inadequate for the needs of the district. He also reported that a suggestion had been made that a station should be erected at Stormstown Junction to cater for the needs of the Ynysybwl branch and provide relief for Aberdare Junction station.

It will be helpful, at this point, briefly to recap the history of Aberdare Junction. A station had opened at Navigation House on 8th October, 1840, and had served as the temporary terminus of the TVR until the opening through to Merthyr the following year. Renamed 'Aberdare Junction' in 1849, the station was originally situated at the foot of the Main Incline. With the replacement of the incline between 1864 and 1867, a new, albeit temporary, station was erected to the south of the junction with the Aberdare branch. On 19th September, 1874 authority was given to erect a more permanent structure, in brick with a verandah on four sides. This had been completed by 12th July, 1877, when the TVR Board resolved to charge the cost of the new station (£1,532 16s. 3d.) to the reserve fund for the renewal of stations.

At the opening of the Ynysybwl branch to passengers in 1890, Aberdare Junction station possessed a somewhat anachronistic layout which was not entirely conducive to efficient train working. The station itself comprised a single island platform on which were located all passenger facilities. This simple arrangement was in marked contrast to the complicated track layout at the junction. This was laid out so that all up and down Merthyr line trains, together with up Aberdare trains, would use the eastern side of the island platform; down through and terminating Aberdare trains ran into the western side of the platform, although it was also possible for such trains to make use of the eastern side. Ynysybwl branch trains arrived at the eastern side of the platform, then ran forward on to the Aberdare branch passenger line where the locomotive ran round its train, before proceeding to a holding siding alongside the Aberdare line, to await the arrival of the train from Aberdare. After this had departed, the Ynysybwl train ran forward to the western side of the platform to pick up passengers and await its own departure time.

By 1895 this archaic layout had become a considerable liability, and on 29th October the TVR Traffic Committee ordered the preparation of plans for improvements at Aberdare Junction, at an estimated cost of £8,170. The new works were notified as ready for Board of Trade inspection on 26th March, 1897, and were inspected by Lt Colonel Yorke. In his report, dated 14th April, 1897, Yorke noted that the island platform had been lengthened and that further improvements were envisaged, including the erection of a new booking office, use of the existing booking office as a waiting room, and the provision of an overall canopy. His main concern, however, was the track layout, which had been altered to enable the mode of working to be rationalised. Under the revised arrangements all up and down Aberdare and up Merthyr trains were kept to the western side of the island platform, while down Merthyr line trains had sole use of the eastern side. Ynysybwl branch trains now arrived on the western side, before proceeding to the holding siding to await the arrival and departure of the Aberdare train. Departure for Ynysybwl was then from the western side of the platform. A new signal box had been provided at the northern end of the station, while the old box was retained at the southern end. Yorke felt that an additional platform was desirable, but acknowledged that limitations on space at the junction prevented this. As the new arrangements were a distinct improvement on the old, he concluded his report by recommending that sanction be granted for the alterations.

This rearrangement was accompanied by a change in the station's name. On 27th October, 1896 the Traffic Committee agreed to change the name from Aberdare Junction to 'Abercynon', to bring it into line with that used by the Post Office and the urban district council. The renaming took effect from 1st December, 1896. Further improvements were initiated on 28th September, 1897 when the Traffic Committee approved the provision of the additional facilities mentioned in Lt Colonel Yorke's report, at an estimated cost of £3,869.

Despite the undoubted improvement produced by these alterations, the use of Abercynon as the junction station for the Ynysybwl branch passenger service suffered from a fairly fundamental disadvantage. Although it offered the possibility of connecting services to Merthyr and Aberdare, this was of little interest to the inhabitants of Ynysybwl, for whom the town of Pontypridd, with its busy market and other delights, was the main attraction. A journey starting

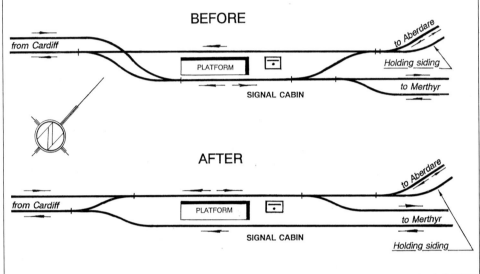

TAFF VALE RAILWAY
REARRANGEMENT OF LINES AT
ABERCYNON 1897
(DIAGRAM OF PASSENGER
LINES ONLY)

BEFORE

from Cardiff

PLATFORM

SIGNAL CABIN

to Aberdare

Holding siding

to Merthyr

AFTER

from Cardiff

PLATFORM

SIGNAL CABIN

to Aberdare

to Merthyr

Holding siding

T. V. Railway Station

Abercynon

Abercynon station *c.* 1905, with a train in the up side of the island platform and a down train from Merthyr approaching.   *Ian Pope Collection*

Abercynon station *c.* 1910, with a couple of TVR class 'K' 0-6-0 tender engines in the foreground.
Lens of Sutton

Work progressing on the Clydach Court Loop, near Clydach Court Junction *c.* 1899.
Welsh Industrial & Maritime Museum

with a lengthy detour, in the wrong direction, and involving an often protracted wait for the connection at Abercynon, was hardly an enticing prospect, and, not surprisingly, a flourishing competitive service of horse brakes grew up on the direct road between Ynysybwl and Pontypridd.

A direct train service between Ynysybwl and Pontypridd required the construction of a south curve between the branch and the main line, near Glyncoch. Such a curve had featured in the TVR Act of 1873, but had been abandoned in 1878. In November 1887 the TVR Solicitor was instructed to prepare notices for a Bill, including such a curve, but this particular aspect had not been proceeded with. Plans for the 'Clydach Court Loop' were eventually deposited in November 1893. It was intended to cater for direct passenger trains between Ynysybwl and Pontypridd, together with the more efficient working of coal traffic from Lady Windsor Colliery.

This last point was a particularly important consideration in view of the fact that the East Glamorgan Railway Bill, promoted in the same Session, included a spur line to serve Lady Windsor Colliery. However, early in the Parliamentary progress of this Bill, its promoters admitted that this short line served no pit which was not already served by the TVR, and on the third day of the inquiry by the House of Lords Committee, the Chairman, Lord Balfour, announced that the committee had decided unanimously against this feature. The rest of the Bill was subsequently rejected by Parliament, leaving only the 'Clydach Court Loop' to be authorised by the TVR Act of 17th August, 1894.

It was not until 1898 that work started on the Clydach Court Loop. On 10th January application was made for Board of Trade sanction for a siding, at Clydach Court, to serve the new works. This was to be connected to the up main line by a trailing connection, controlled by a ground frame. This did not satisfy the Board of Trade, however, with the result that a signal box and full signalling were required. Wagons were set down and picked up by goods trains in the up direction only.

It was originally intended that the Clydach Court Loop would join the Ynysybwl branch at a new junction at the convergence of the two lines, about ½ mile from Clydach Court Junction. However, on 30th May, 1899, the Traffic Committee agreed to extend the new line to run parallel with the Ynysybwl branch to Windsor Passing Siding. On completion, the two single lines created the impression of a double line from their meeting point to the actual junction.

John Aird & Co. were the contractors for the works, which proceeded without incident. On 21st May, 1900 Clydach Court Junction was stated to be ready for Board of Trade inspection, and was reported on by Colonel Yorke on 25th May, 1900. A double junction had been installed in the main line, together with trailing sidings on the up side. The junction was controlled by a new signal box, containing 35 levers, of which 28 were in use. In conjunction with the provision of the new junction, a short section of the main line, which had passed through a reverse curve at this point, had been straightened out.

At the other end of the Clydach Court Loop, Board of Trade approval had been sought in August 1899 for alterations at Windsor Passing Siding. The original proposal involved the retention of the up and down passing loop, with a scissors crossover forming the junction between Ynysybwl branch and the line from Clydach Court Junction. However, the Board of Trade refused to approve this layout because of the severe gradients on the approaches to the junction. As a result, the signalling arrangements were altered to create an up and down loop siding for goods and mineral traffic only, with the other line acting as the up and down main line. The new junction was ready for Board of Trade inspection on 21st May, 1900, and was inspected by Colonel Yorke on the same day that he inspected Clydach Court Junction. Yorke recommended approval for the new works, provided the loop siding was not used by passenger trains.

The line between the two junctions was not submitted for inspection, however, an omission that did not auger well for the early introduction of a direct passenger train service between Ynysybwl and Pontypridd.

The Clydach Court Loop under construction, from the site of the later Clydach Court Platform, c. 1899.   *Welsh Industrial & Maritime Museum*

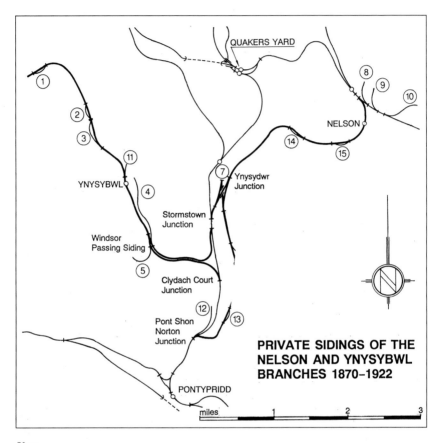

PRIVATE SIDINGS OF THE
NELSON AND YNYSYBWL
BRANCHES 1870–1922

Key

Collieries
1. Llanwonno.
2. Black Grove.
3. Mynachdy.
4. Lady Windsor.
5. Darranddu / Great Western.
6. Albion.
7, Dowlais-Cardiff.
8. Llancaiach.
9. Top Hill.
10. Gelligaer.

Quarries
11. Ynysybwl.
12. Graig-yr-Hesg.
13. Taylor's.
14. Whitehall.
15. Berthgron.

Not all sidings co-existed.

Chapter Six

The Nelson and Ynysybwl Branches, 1900-1922

On 18th January, 1900 John Aird & Co., having completed the contracts on the Clydach Court and Cilfynydd Loops, held an auction sale of material used in the construction of these lines. This event was regarded, at the time, as being of some significance, heralding the prospect of the early introduction of direct passenger trains between the Nelson and Ynysybwl branches and Pontypridd. However, no indication had been given as to when such services would commence and the opening of the new loop lines was only part of the story. The introduction of direct passenger trains was not a straightforward matter, given the inadequate facilities at Pontypridd and the serious and growing congestion at that station. At this date the layout at Pontypridd was basically that created as a result of major alterations carried out in the 1860s. There were through platforms each side of the up and down running lines, together with a bay platform serving the Rhondda branch and another at the Cardiff end of the station added in 1888 to provide accommodation for PC&NR trains. With such limited facilities, the TVR was prepared to introduce only one additional passenger train service, and selected that between Nelson and Pontypridd. As a result, despite the completion of the Clydach Court Loop in 1900, passengers from Ynysybwl, wishing to travel to Pontypridd, continued to be faced with frustrating delays awaiting connections at Abercynon.

Rebuilding of Pontypridd station had been an ambition of the TVR since the early 1890s. The station site was very confined and land acquisition for expansion a very expensive and protracted process. The work at the station was carried out in two stages: the first involved the provision of relief goods and mineral lines, while the second covered rebuilding of the passenger accommodation. Considerable relief came with segregation of the mineral traffic in the early 1900s. One of the mineral lines (temporarily used by both up and down traffic) was brought into use on 4th December, 1900, the other being reported as ready for Board of Trade inspection on 17th October, 1901. With two mineral lines available, normal up and down working was instituted. However, these lines provided relief only for Rhondda branch traffic. The next step was to install a double line connection from the Merthyr line to the relief lines, crossing the Rhondda branch and bay line, in the process. This was reported to be ready for inspection on 18th September, 1902. In addition, a new signal box was erected at Pontypridd Junction, containing 135 levers, of which no less than 54 were spare, an indication of the scale of the changes yet to come.

The passenger train service between Nelson and Pontypridd was introduced on 1st June, 1900, with intermediate stations opened at Cilfynydd and Coedpenmaen. At first, goods facilities were limited to those already existing at Nelson, then still used by the GWR for its Llancaiach goods traffic, but on 25th September, 1900, the TVR Traffic Committee agreed to provide such accommodation at Cilfynydd. The goods station at Cilfynydd opened on 15th April, 1901. Another proposal for an additional station, this time for

Nelson Station (GWR), *c.* 1905. The Nelson branch joined the GWR Pontypool Road-Neath line just behind the station building. *E. Evans Collection*

A panoramic view of Ynysybwl station, *c.* 1905, with an 0-6-2T engine and four-wheeled coaches at the platform. *Lens of Sutton*

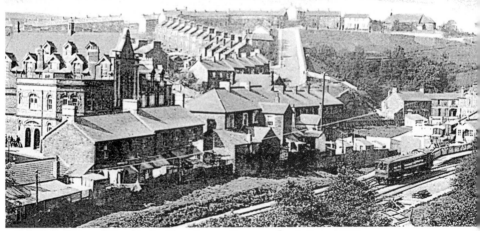

A general view of Ynysybwl with a steam railcar near the station, *c.* 1910.
Welsh Industrial & Maritime Museum

passengers, was considered by the Traffic Committee on 16th July, 1900, when an application for a workmen's train service between Nelson and Dowlais-Cardiff Colliery, Abercynon, was reported. A station was required at Travellers' Rest, at a convenient point for the colliery, and this was approved, at an estimated cost of £1,000, together with the introduction of the workmen's service. On 12th March, 1901, the committee was informed that the new station would be ready for opening on 18th March, 1901. Whether or not his date was met is unclear, as Clinker gives the opening date of Travellers' Rest station as 1st May, 1901.

Meanwhile, on the Ynysybwl branch, early hopes that the completion of the Clydach Court Loop would lead to the introduction of a direct service of passenger trains at Pontypridd were soon frustrated, and the new line was restricted to goods and mineral traffic only. Pressure for improved facilities did not cease, however. In February 1902 local residents petitioned for an improved service, but had to be content with an additional train, on Saturdays only. On 21st November, 1903 a deputation from Pontypridd and Ynysybwl met TVR General Manager Ammon Beasley to air a number of grievances, including the need for the rebuilding of Pontypridd passenger station and the introduction of a direct service from Ynysybwl. When this meeting was reported to the Traffic Committee on 15th December, 1903, it was agreed to consider the running of such a service when the new station at Pontypridd was completed, or when a steam railcar service could be provided. Clearly, a new station was some way off, but in December 1903 a steam railcar or 'Motor car' (to use the TVR terminology) service was a distinct possibility.

Motor car No. 1 had been completed in October 1903 and, after a number of trial runs, was introduced on an experimental service on the Penarth branch. One of the reasons for employing such vehicles was to counter the threat of competition from existing or projected street tramways. This consideration was particularly relevant in the case of the Nelson branch, as in 1900 an unsuccessful attempt had been made to obtain powers for a tramway from Pontypridd to Cilfynydd. Indeed, this scheme may well have influenced the TVR's decision to introduce a passenger service on the Nelson branch despite the obvious difficulties in accommodating such a service at Pontypridd station. In October 1900 Mr R.P. Wilson, consulting electrical engineer to Pontypridd Urban District Council, recommended that the council seek tramway powers, including a line from Pontypridd to Cilfynydd. This was agreed and an application was made for a Provisional Order under the Tramways Act 1870 in the 1901 Parliamentary Session. This application was strenuously opposed by the TVR on the grounds that it, as a major ratepayer, would, in effect, be subsidising competition for its own services. This argument did not impress, however, and the tramway scheme was authorised on 17th August, 1901, with services being introduced on 5th March, 1905.

Following the successful operation of the motor car service on the Penarth branch, the TVR proceeded to introduce similar services throughout its system. On 26th April, 1904 the Traffic Committee gave consideration to proposals for stopping places for the cars at various locations on the proposed routes. At this stage, the company was undecided between ground level and raised platforms

Tramcars, including one destined for Cilfynydd, at the depot at Treforest on the official opening day, 5th March, 1905.

Pontypridd Library

TVR Motor Car (locomotive unit No. 9) and its proud crew at Old Ynysybwl *c.* 1905.

R.F. Wilding

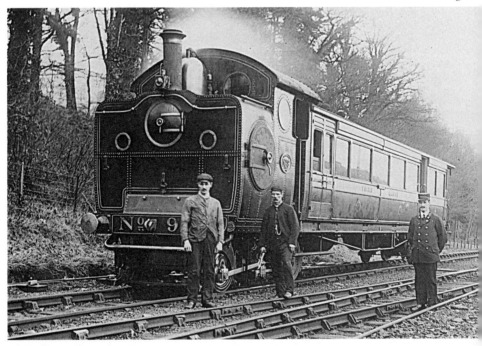

for the cars and left the choice to the Chairman, after he had had the opportunity of assessing the operation of the folding steps fitted to Car No. 1. 'Platforms', as they were always known by the TVR, were proposed at Abernant on the Nelson branch and Berw Road (main line) and Robertstown between Pontypridd and Ynysybwl, and at Old Ynysybwl. The Chairman was clearly not satisfied with the folding steps as on 10th May, 1904 the Traffic Committee approved amended plans for raised platforms at the suggested stopping places.

The introduction of the motor car service on the Ynysybwl branch involved the upgrading to passenger standard of the freight-only lines between Ynysybwl station and Old Ynysybwl and between Clydach Court Junction and Windsor Passing Siding. Both sections were inspected by Colonel Druitt, whose report to the Board of Trade, dated 7th July, 1904, stated:

I have now inspected the following railways about to be opened for passenger traffic by the Taff Vale Railway.

I) The Ynysybwl South Curve, a single line 36.17 chains in length constructed under the TVR Act of 1894 commencing by a double junction with the Company's main line at Clydach Court Junction and terminating by single junction with a pair of rails now brought into use for passenger traffic, a doubling of the Ynysybwl branch line originally built under the Act of 1873.

II) This new pair of rails is 50.25 chains in length and starts at Windsor Siding Signal Box by a junction with the original single line which is already opened for passenger traffic. No alterations have been made at the junction boxes concerned. Clydach Court Junction Box now contains 29 working and 6 spare levers and Windsor Siding Box 38 working and 4 spare levers. There is one underbridge on the above section, viz over the Clydach river, consisting of steel plate girders and troughing and of a skew span of 70 ft. These girders and troughing gave moderate deflections under test load and appear to be of sufficient theoretical strength. This line which is about to be opened for motor carriage traffic is worked on the Electric Train Staff method and the Company should forward the usual undertaking to that effect.

The permanent way is in good order of the TVR standard section as described in the schedule forwarded by the Company, and I can recommend the Board of Trade to sanction the use of the above lines for passenger traffic.

I have also inspected, at the request of the Company:

III) A further section of the same Ynysybwl single branch line 40.25 chains in length commencing at Ynysybwl station and terminating at a new motor carriage platform at Old Ynysybwl. The line from Windsor Siding Signal Box to the station was inspected and passed for traffic in 1889. There is one river bridge on this new section consisting of masonry abutments and piers and two spans of timber baulks under each rail with timber corbels 3 in. long. These gave moderate deflections under test load and have sufficient theoretical strength. Skew span 26 ft 9 in.

The top ballasting is not completed and the points of the siding and the trap points in the mineral line beyond Old Ynysybwl Platform require to be controlled by the Train Staff of the section Ynysybwl-Llanwonno. This section is to be worked by one engine in steam (or 2 coupled together) and the usual undertaking to that effect should be forwarded by the Company. The Platform at Old Ynysybwl is 40 ft long, 10 ft wide by 3 ft high and a gate is required as pointed out on the spot with the Company to prevent access to the platform except by the authorised path.

No alteration has been made in the interlocking at Ynysybwl Signal Box, but a longer locking bar is required at the facing point just beyond the station to suit the length

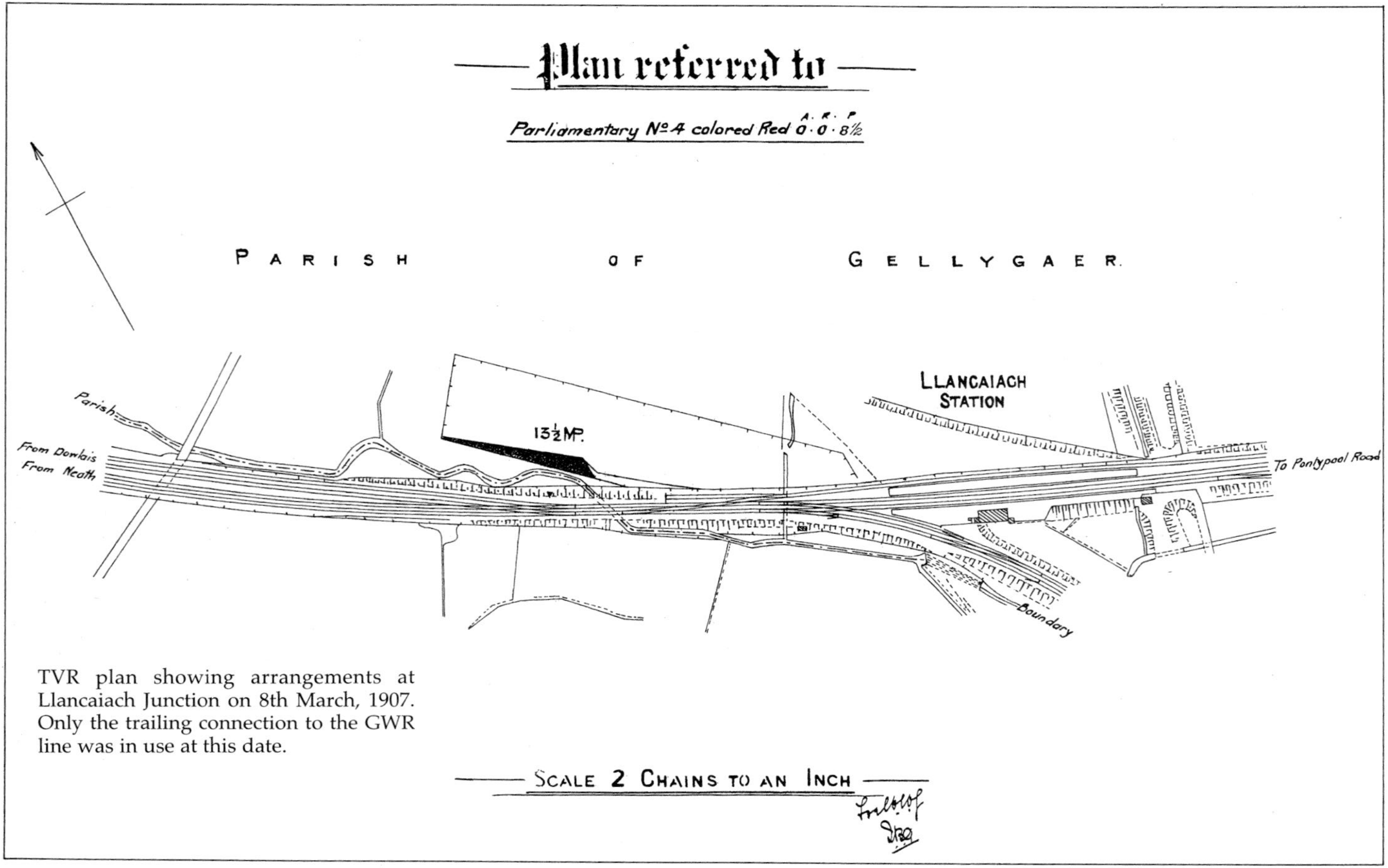

Plan referred to

Parliamentary Nº 4 colored Red 0·0·8½

PARISH   OF   GELLYGAER.

LLANCAIACH STATION

15¾ MP.

To Pontypool Road

Boundary

Parish

From Dowlais
From Neath

SCALE 2 CHAINS TO AN INCH

TVR plan showing arrangements at Llancaiach Junction on 8th March, 1907. Only the trailing connection to the GWR line was in use at this date.

between the wheels of the motor cars. It now contains 23 working and 2 spare levers. The platform at Old Ynysybwl being only 40 ft long is of course unsuited to ordinary trains.

Subject to the completion of the above requirements, which should be reported to the Company, I can recommend the Board of Trade to sanction this further section of the Ynysybwl branch line for passenger traffic by Motor Cars.

The motor car service between Pontypridd and Nelson was the first of the two to be introduced, on 10th October, 1904. The inaugural car arrived at Nelson at 9.30 am, accompanied by Oscar Hurford, station master at Pontypridd, and other railway officials. A large crowd awaited the car's arrival, which was announced by the detonation of numerous fog signals. The platform at Llanfabon Road (Abernant) opened the same day.

A week later, on 17th October, 1904, the Ynysybwl motor car service was introduced, running via the Clydach Court Loop. The first car arrived at Ynysybwl at 7.20 am amid a salvo of the customary fog signals. Owing to the early hour and the 'wretched' weather conditions, few passengers availed themselves of this first trip, but the departure for Pontypridd was well-filled. Once again responsibility for the arrangements fell to Oscar Hurford, who was accompanied, on this occasion, by W.H. Evans of the Traffic Office, chief permanent way inspector Davies, permanent way inspector Carsdale and locomotive inspector Parry. The motorman was H.L. Davies, the assistant motorman J.W. Jenkins and the conductor W. Lewis. One consequence of the introduction of the new service was the withdrawal of that between Ynysybwl and Abercynon, but this does not appear to have been a source of great regret or even comment in the locality.

It was not until 29th October, 1904 that Colonel Druitt reported on the motor car platforms at Berw Road and Robertstown, on the route of the Ynysybwl service, and Llanfabon Road on the Nelson line. Berw Road consisted of platforms alongside the up and down main lines, mid-way between Pont Shon Norton and Clydach Court Junctions, and linked by ramps to the nearby road overbridge. The other platforms were single line only. All were 40 ft long with a width of 9 to 10 ft, and lacked any form of shelter. Intending passengers were confined to a fenced enclosure, clear of the platform, until admitted to the platform itself by the conductor on the arrival of the car.

The motor cars proved very popular and soon gave rise to requests for additional stopping places and improved facilities, wherever they were introduced. However, early pleas for such platforms did not meet with much success. On 6th December, 1904 a request for a platform at New Road on the Ynysybwl branch was rejected, as was one for St Cynon's Church, on the Nelson branch, which was turned down on 26th September, 1905. One feature which certainly was not popular was the absence of any form of shelter at the platforms. Initially, the TVR appears to have been reluctant to accede to such demands, as in the case of a refusal to provide a covering and seating at Llanfabon Road Platform in October 1905. Other types of improvement proved less objectionable, however; on 22nd May, 1906 authority was given for an extension to Llanfabon Road Platform, presumably to enable trains, as well as cars, to call there.

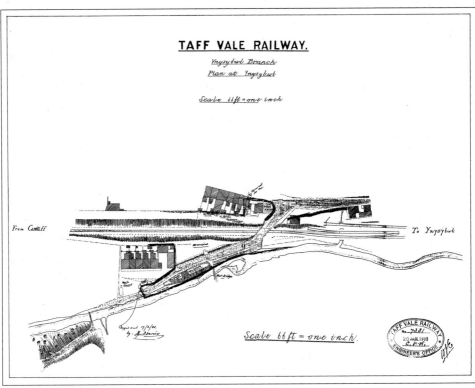

TVR plan showing the southern approach to Ynysybwl station, 20th January, 1903.

The Nelson branch train and station staff pose for the camera at the branch terminus, *c.* 1905.
E. Evans Collection

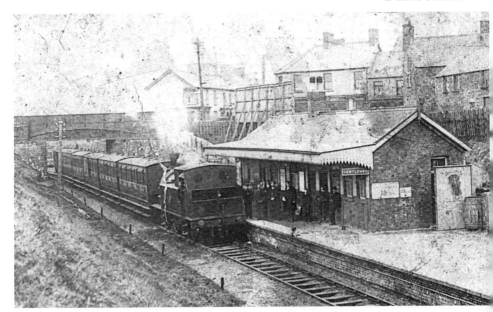

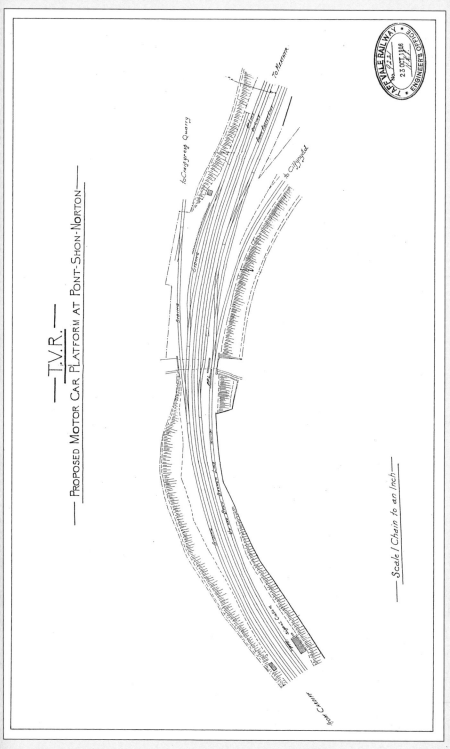

— T.V.R. —

— PROPOSED MOTOR CAR PLATFORM AT PONT-SHON-NORTON —

To Merthyr

to Craig-yr-eos Quarry

to Cilfynydd

To Cardiff

— Scale 1 Chain to an Inch —

TVR plan of Pont Shon Norton Junction, 23rd October, 1906, prepared in connection with the relocation of Berw Road Platform, but, contrary to its heading, not showing the site of the platform.

☞ TOURIST TICKETS

(AVAILABLE FOR SIX MONTHS)

ARE ISSUED DAILY (except Sundays) FROM

PONTYPRIDD.

TO	FARES via Cardiff		TO	FARES via Cardiff		FARES, via Aberdare. Do not include conveyance between the Stations in Aberdare	
	1st Class	3rd Class		1st Class	3rd Class	1st Class	3rd Class
	s. d.	s. d.		s. d.	s. d.	s. d.	s. d.
Bath	18 2	10 6	Truro or Newquay ...	67 11	36 9	...	...
Clevedon	18 2	11 6	Falmouth, Penryn, Perranporth, or St. Agnes ...	70 5	38 0	...	...
Weston-super-Mare ...	19 8	11 9					
Watchet	32 6	19 0	Penzance, St. Ives, or Helston ...	74 8	41 0	...	...
Minehead	35 0	20 0					
Dulverton	33 11	19 0	Scilly Isles	85 2	48 6	...	...
Barnstaple	40 8	23 3	Winchester	38 8	22 3	...	...
Ilfracombe (L. & S.W.)	45 1	25 3	Dorchester	35 2	20 0	...	...
†Exeter	36 8	21 0	Weymouth	37 2	21 0	...	...
Dawlish	40 4	22 3	Bridport	35 8	20 0	...	...
Starcross	39 2	22 3	Guernsey or Jersey— Saloon on Steamer ...	61 8	45 9	...	...
Teignmouth	41 2	23 3	2nd Cabin ,, ...	...	35 9	...	...
Torquay,Paignton, Bovey or Chudleigh § via Newton Abbot	42 8	24 3	Ferryside	23 6	13 9	17 6	9 6
			Carmarthen	25 8	13 9	20 0	11 9
Newton Abbot ...	42 0	23 3	Llandyssil	31 0	17 0	24 10	13 9
Totnes or Moreton Hampstead ...	45 2	25 3	Newcastle Emlyn ...	33 0	18 0	26 7	14 9
Ashburton, Brixham, Dartmouth, or Buckfastleigh	47 2	25 3	Tenby, Saundersfoot or Haverfordwest	34 2	19 0	28 10	15 9
Plymouth, Devonport, Princetown, Tavistock or Kingsbridge (via Brent)... ...	50 10	27 6	Milford Haven ... Neyland ... Pembroke ... Pembroke Dock... Cardigan ... Fishguard and Goodwick ...	36 11	20 0	31 1	17 0
Liskeard *	57 5	31 6	Aberystwyth, via Pencader	42 2	22 3	33 3	18 0
Wadebridge or Bodmin	61 2	33 9	Swansea	...	...	10 10	6 6
Fowey or St. Austell ...	62 8	34 9	Lampeter for Aberayron	33 10	18 0	...	...

From PENARTH to ABERYSTWITH, via Cardiff (G.W.R.) 1st Class 38/6, 3rd Class 20/-
For General Conditions, &c., see Great Western Railway Company's Programme, which may be obtained at the Booking Office, Pontypridd. See also next page for breaks of journey, &c.

    *Looe.—Tourist Tickets for Looe via Liskeard are issued at fares—2s. 6d. 1st Class ; and 1s. 3rd Class above the fares for Liskeard.

    §Chudleigh via Exeter and Ide.—Tickets available via Exeter and Ide are issued at fares—4s. 6d. 1st Class and 2s. 3rd Class, above the fares for Exeter.

    †Christow.—Tourist Tickets for Christow via Exeter are issued at fares: 2/10 1st class, and 1/5 3rd class above the fares for Exeter.

Extract from TVR excursion arrangements 1909.

Considerable disruption resulted when, on 28th November, 1905, a motor car from Nelson left the rails, near Pont Shon Norton Junction. There were only three passengers on board at the time and none were injured. The Nelson service was suspended for the rest of the day, while that to Ynysybwl worked from Abercynon. The line was reopened late that evening.

The early years of the present century saw further growth in coal traffic on the TVR main line, resulting in increased congestion on the double track section between Stormstown Junction and Pont Shon Norton Junction. On 24th April, 1906 the Traffic Committee was presented with plans and estimates for a down relief line from Clydach Court Junction to Pont Shon Norton Junction, where it was to join the existing relief line to Pontypridd Northern Junction. This proposal was accepted and the works ordered to be carried out, at an estimated cost of £5,290. In conjunction with this work, it was necessary to remove Berw Road Platform and the committee recommended that it be relocated on the Pont Shon Norton branch, at an estimated cost of £82.

The new relief line was opened on 8th October, 1906, Berw Road Platform having been closed by 1st June, 1906. It was not until 12th November, 1906, however, that the new connections at Clydach Court and Pont Shon Norton Junctions were reported on by Colonel Druitt, for the Board of Trade. At Clydach Court Junction the down relief line left the down main line shortly before the junction with the Ynysybwl line. A facing crossover just beyond the junction enabled trains from the Ynysybwl branch to reach the relief line. At Pont Shon Norton Junction the relief line joined the single track branch, trains running over a short section of it to reach the existing relief line, a movement which required special signalling precautions. A crossover road, just before the junction, allowed trains to leave the relief line for the main line at this point.

In spite of clear instructions having been given to relocate Berw Road Platform, nothing appears to have been done in the matter until 29th January, 1907, when the Traffic Committee received a Memorial from the inhabitants of Berw Road and the adjoining area pressing for the platform to be provided at Lewis Terrace, off Berw Road. Obviously embarrassed by this lack of action, the Committee ordered that this request be acceded to, without further delay. However, at its meeting on 28th May, 1907 the Committee was informed that it had been found that the only access to the site at Lewis Terrace was by means of a private road owned by Lord Tredegar, whose agent refused to grant such a right. Further investigations produced an alternative site on the branch line just beyond Pont Shon Norton Junction, and this was approved by the Committee on 11th June, 1907. The relocated facility was inspected by Colonel Druitt on 27th February, 1908, and comprised a single platform 40 ft in length, approached by a ramp from the adjoining public road. Approval was granted, subject to the platform being used only by single motor cars.

At Pontypridd the Nelson and Ynysybwl cars ran into the down main line platform. Such branch line services could also depart from this platform, making use of a single slip in the crossing of the up main line by the down Rhondda line. Facing point locks had been installed in 1900, bringing these connections up to an appropriate standard for passenger service use. The provision of separate lines for mineral trains earlier in the decade had produced

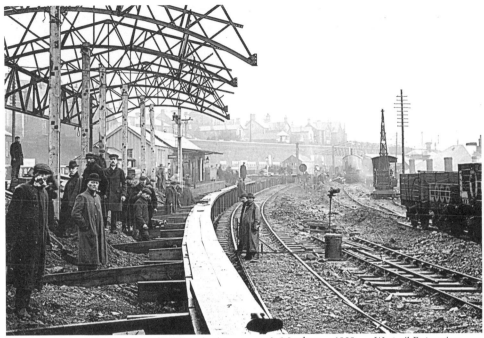

Pontypridd station during rebuilding, looking towards Merthyr, *c.* 1908.　　*Westrail Enterprises*

The through passenger lines at Pontypridd, showing the scale of disruption involved during the rebuilding of the passenger facilities.　　*Westrail Enterprises*

CHRISTMAS HOLIDAYS.

— ON —

Monday, December 27th,

AN

EXCURSION TRAIN

WILL BE RUN TO

SWANSEA

Via Treherbert and Rhondda and Swansea Bay Railway, as under:—

Leaving	Times of Departure	3rd Class Return Fares	Leaving	Times of Departure	3rd Class Return Fares
	a.m.			a.m.	
CARDIFF (Queen St.)	9 15		PONTYPRIDD	9 40	
			TREHAFOD	9 45	3s. 0d.
LLANDAFF	9 20		PORTH	9 55	
RADYR	9 25	3s. 3d.			
TAFFS WELL	9 30		MAERDY	8 20	
TREFOREST	9 35		FERNDALE	8 25	3s. 0d.
			TYLORSTOWN	8 30	
NELSON	7 45		YNYSHIR	8 35	
TRAVELLER'S REST ..	7 50	3s. 3d.	DINAS	10 0	
(Abercynon Upper)			Tonypandy and Trealaw	10 5	
CILFYNYDD	7 55		LLWYNYPIA	10 10	2s. 9d.
			YSTRAD	10 15	
			TREORCHY	10 20	

Passengers from the Nelson Section change trains at Pontypridd. and passengers from the Ferndale Section at Porth in both directions.

The RETURN TRAIN will leave SWANSEA (R. & S. B. Rly.) Station at 8.0 p.m. the same day.

Children under 12 years of age half-price.   No luggage allowed.

TVR Christmas Holidays Excursions 1909.

NELSON SECTION. WEEKDAYS. [20

UP.

		a.m	a.m		a.m	a.m	a.m	p.m	p.m	p.m	p.m	p.m	p.m	
Connecting Trains arr. Pontypridd —		W	T		Car	Car	Car	Car	T	Car	Car	Car	Car	
From Rhondda at ..					8 17	9 49	11 2	1 39	2 45	4 5	6 7	8 8	9 38	
" Cardiff "		4 44			8 34	9 42	11 9	1 42	2 49	4 24	6 27	8 4	10 9	Saturdays only.
" Cowbridge "					8 9	9 23	11 1	1 21	..	4 14	5 57	7 59	9 32	
Pontypridd	dep.	4 48	6 30	..	8 45	10 0	1125	1 51	2 55	5 3	6 38	8 30	1027	
Berw Road	"				8 48	10 3	1128	1 54		5 6	6 41	8 33	1030	
Coedpenmaen	"	4 52	6 34	..	8 50	10 5	1130	1 56	3 0	5 8	6 43	8 35	1032	
Cilfynydd	"	4 58	6 38		8 54	10 9	1134	2 0	3 4	5 12	6 47	8 39	1036	
Traveller's Rest ..	"	5 3	6 43	...	9 0	1015	1140	2 6	3 10	5 18	6 53	8 45	1042	
Llanfabon Road Platform	"	5 8	6 48		9 7	1022	1147	2 13	3 17	5 25	7 0	8 52	1049	
Nelson	arr.	5 10	6 50	..	9 9	1024	1149	2 15	3 19	5 27	7 2	8 54	1052	

DOWN.

		a.m	a.m	a.m	a.m		p.m	p.m	pm.	p.m	p.m	p.m	p.m	
		W	T	Car	Car		Car	CarA	T	Car	Car	Car	Car	
Nelson	dep.	5 20	7 48	9 18	1033	..	1243	2 19	3 53	5 61	7 28	9 0	11 3	
Llanfabon Road Platform	"	5 22	7 50	9 20	1035	..	1245	2 21	3 55	5 53	7 30	9 2	11 5	Saturdays only. On Thursdays & Sats at 1-14 p.m
Traveller's Rest ..	"	5 27	7 55	9 27	1042	...	1252	2 28	4 2	6 0	7 37	9 0	1111	
Cilfynydd .	"	5 32	8 0	9 32	1047		1257	2 33	4 7	6 5	7 42	9 14	1115	
Coedpenmaen	"	5 36	8 4	9 36	1051	...	1 1	2 37	4 11	6 9	7 46	9 18	1119	
Berw Road	"			9 38	1053		1 3	2 39		6 11	7 48	9 20	1121	
Pontypridd	arr.	5 40	8 8	9 40	1055	..	1 5	2 41	4 15	6 13	7 50	9 22	1123	
Connecting Trains leave Pontypridd														
For Rhondda at ..		5 43	8 38	9 45	1123	..	1 33	2 52	4 32	6 8 30	8 8	9 44	1140	
" Cardiff "		6 59	8 20	9 54	11 5		1 23	2 49	4 29	6 8 59	8 4	9 44	1134	
" Cowbridge "			8 33	10 0	1125	...	1 48	3 12	5 10	6 25	8 18	10 5	..	

§-For Passengers holding Ordinary Tickets only from Pontypridd.   A-A carriage for Workmen will be attached daily.   T-Train.   W-Workmen.   Not run Bk. Hdy.

TVR public timetable, July-September 1910.

YNYSYBWL SECTION. WEEKDAYS. [21

UP.

		a m	a.m	a.m	a.m	p.m	p.m	p.m	p.m	p.m		p.m	p.m	p.m	p.m	p.m	p.m	p.m
Conn. Trains arr. Pontypridd																		
From Rhondda at ..		6 57	8 17	9 2	11 2	1227	1 39	2 45	4 5	4 58	..	6 7	6a56	..	8 8	..	9 38	..
" Cardiff at		6 59	8 34	9 42	11 9	1228	1 42	3 24	4 24		..	6 9	6a27	7a44	8 15	..	10 9	11a14
" Merthyr at			8 25	9 6	1113	..	1 21	2 46	4 26	..	..	6 19	..	..	8 2	..	9 41	11a 1
" Aberdare at			8 25	9 40	1113	1223	1 21	2 46	4 26	5 20		6 19	6a51		8 2	..	9 41	..
" Cowbridge at			8 9	9 23	11 1		1 21	2 58	4 14	..		5 57	..	..	7 59	...	9 32	
Pontypridd	dep.	7 20	8 43	9 45	1123	1232	1 53	3 3	4 32	5 23		6 25	7a 5	7a53	8 23	9a33	10 24	11a20
Robertstown	"	7 31	8 54	9 56	1134	1243	2 4	3 46	4 45	5 34	..	6 36	7a16	8a 2	8 34	9a42	10 35	11a31
Ynysybwl ..	"	7 34	8 57	9 59	1137	1246	2 7	3 49	4 46	5 37	..	6 39	7a19	8a 5	8 37	9a45	10 38	11a34
Old Ynysybwl	arr.	7 36	8 59	10 1	1139	1249	2 9	3 51	4 48	5 39	..	6*41	7a21	..	8 39	..	1C 40	11a36

DOWN.

		a.m	a.m	p.m	p.m	p.m	p.m	p.m	p.m		p.m	p.m	p.m	p.m	p.m	p.m	p.m
Old Ynysybwl	dep.	7 47	9 5	1034	12 4	1259	2 20	4 4	4 49	..	5 49	..	7 34	..	9 2	..	10 49
Ynysybwl ..	"	7 50	9 8	1037	12 7	1 2	2 23	4 7	4 52		5 52	6a47	7 37	8a 8	9 5	9a50	10 52
Robertstown	"	7 53	9 11	1040	1210	1 5	2 26	4 10	4 58		5 55	6a50	7 40	8a11	9 8	9a53	10 55
Pontypridd	arr.	8 3	9 21	1050	1220	1 15	2 36	4 20	5 5		6 5	7a 0	7 50	8a21	9 18	10a8	11 5
Conn. Trains leave Pontyp'd																a	
For Cardiff at		8 20	9 54	11 5	1230	1 23	2 49	4 29	5 48	..	6 9	..	8 4	..	9 44	1024	11 34
" Rhondda "		8 38	9 45	1123	1230	1 33	2 52	4 32	5 46		6 30	7a46	8	8a52	9 44	1013	11†40
" Aberdare "		8 12	9 33	1118	1240	1 47	3 28	4 27	5 10		6 12	..	8 17	..	10 12	1012	11 33
" Merthyr "		8 26	9 33	1118	1235	1 47	3 28	4 27	6 12		6 12	..	8 17		10 12	1012	11 33
" Cowbridge "		8 31	10 0	1125	b	1 48	3 12	..	5 10		6 25	..	8 18	..	10	5 10a5	..

*—On Sats. will run to Ynysybwl only.   a—Sats. only.   †—On Sats at 11-18 pm.
b—Merthyr arrive 12-35 p.m.   From July 23rd to September 10th only.

The new Nelson & Llancaiach station on the GWR, shortly after its opening in 1912.
T.J. McCarthy Collection

considerable relief at the station, but there remained a pressing need for improved accommodation for passenger services. On 7th November, 1905 approval was given by the Traffic Committee to a plan of the new station layout, together with authority to seek tenders for the platform covering. Instructions to proceed with the work of altering the platform arrangements at Pontypridd were given on 19th December, 1906. The original plan comprised a single island platform with two inset bays at the Merthyr end of the station, one for the Rhondda line and the other for cars from Nelson and Ynysybwl, together with a similar bay at the Cardiff end. Work proceeded on this basis, but on 15th January, 1909, it was agreed to insert two short motor car bays at the Merthyr end of the station. At the inspection of the works on 12th October, 1909, it was noted that the new bays were nearing completion, whilst on 28th February, 1910 they were recorded as open and in use. The new down main line platform, used by all down Merthyr and Rhondda through trains, opened on 7th March, 1910, together with the bay at the Cardiff end, used by GWR trains from Caerphilly and Newport.

On 13th May, 1912 the new works were inspected by Colonel Druitt, who noted that the track alterations had been completed, but that the buildings were still under construction. Two years later, on 28th July, 1914, the TVR Directors inspected the last building to be completed at the new station, the ladies' waiting room. In addition, the fixing of gates and railings at the station approach had been carried out. As a result, the Engineer was able to report that the reconstruction of Pontypridd station was practically completed. It had taken over seven years, involving considerable upheaval, disruption and expense. On 17th November, 1915 Colonel Druitt, having returned to re-inspect the works, completed his final report. The new island platform was 560 yards long, with a maximum width of 66 ft. Of the two short motor car bays at the Merthyr end of the platform, one was connected to the Rhondda branch and the other to the Merthyr line, the latter for use by Ynysybwl services. Nelson trains usually used the inset bay alongside the down main line. A large street level booking office had been provided, with access by subway to the platform. Druitt was clearly impressed with the various facilities, including the waiting and refreshment rooms, and recommended that final approval be given for the new works.

A change to the daily routine of the Nelson branch occurred on 27th June, 1912, when the TVR 'Royal Train', comprising class 'C' 4-4-2T No. 173, the Directors' saloon, a composite coach and passenger brake van, conveyed King George V and Queen Mary over the line *en route* from Cardiff to Dowlais, watched by vast crowds at each of the settlements passed.

The opening of the tramway between Pontypridd and Cilfynydd in 1905 had a dramatic effect on the traffic of the Nelson branch, severely reducing the numbers of passengers using Coedpenmaen and Cilfynydd stations. On 4th December, 1906, the Traffic Committee, responding to this situation, agreed to reduce Coedpenmaen to the status of a motor car platform, a process which involved the removal of staff and building, but not a change in title. However, this economy measure was not sufficient to save Coedpenmaen, and on 13th October, 1914 the Traffic Committee agreed to its closure, which, according to

Abercynon station, looking towards Merthyr, *c.* 1910, with the engine shed visible in the distance on the right of the picture.   *Lens of Sutton*

Clearing up after a mishap at Abercynon in TVR days, with the engine shed in the background.
C.W. Harris Collection

Clinker, took place on 1st June, 1915. Travellers' Rest station also suffered from poor patronage, and on 11th March, 1910, it was decided that it too should be reduced to the status of a motor car platform, again without the indignity of the suffix being added to its title.

Traffic on the Ynysybwl branch grew rapidly after the introduction of the motor cars and direct services to Pontypridd in 1904. Robertstown Platform, in particular, was well-situated for the settlement it was intended to serve, and its success was reflected by the gradual improvement in the accommodation it offered. On 22nd February, 1908 provision of a shelter was approved, and on 30th January, 1917 the Traffic Committee authorised the provision of a booking office at the Platform. Requests for additional stopping places elsewhere on the branch also met with more success. On 14th January, 1910 the Traffic Committee agreed to provide a motor car platform at New Road, just above Windsor Passing Siding, at an estimated cost of £270. Ynysybwl (New Road) Platform opened on 6th July, 1910, and comprised a single platform, 132 ft long, initially without shelter. However, this deficiency was remedied in 1912, following a request from Miss Price, a school mistress at New Road Infants School.

Old Ynysybwl Platform retained the most basic of facilities, until a corrugated iron waiting shed was provided in 1912. In 1915 plans were prepared for the extension of the platform, following an accident in which a passenger had fallen from an auto-trailer, which had stopped short of the platform, but, possibly because of wartime conditions, this was not taken any further.

In December 1914 a request from Rhondda Urban District Council and local residents for a Platform at Clydach Court was rejected, but in the following July the application was reconsidered and approved. Clydach Court Platform was inspected by Colonel Druitt for the Board of Trade on 16th October, 1915, and was 132 ft long, approached by a pathway from an adjoining overbridge.

During 1908 and 1909 consideration was given to the introduction of an additional motor car service between Abercynon and Merthyr. Although approved in principle on 1st January, 1909, nothing came of this proposal, possibly because of reluctance on the part of the TVR to pay the additional rent demanded by the GWR for the use of its Merthyr station by the proposed service. One interesting feature of the proposed service, details of which emerged in June 1909 in a letter written by Ammon Beasley, was the intention to restore the link between Abercynon and Ynysybwl, making use of spare time in the proposed Merthyr-Abercynon motor car timetable. Another, again unsuccessful, proposal appeared at about the same time in connection with negotiations for the absorption of the RR by the TVR, under the latter's Vesting Bill in the 1909 Session. It was proposed to introduce a motor car service between Pontypridd and Dowlais, via the Llancaiach branch. However, with the failure of the Vesting Bill, the incentive for this service faded away, and in February 1910 the TVR Directors decided not to proceed further with this project.

The abandonment of the proposal for a motor car service between Pontypridd and Dowlais paved the way for an agreement between the TVR and the GWR to simplify the junction between the two lines at Llancaiach. A double junction had been installed in 1889, but the facing connection from the GWR had remained bolted out of use, because of the TVR's refusal to contribute

Down Goods and Mineral Trains picking up at Storage Sidings, Pont Shon Norton.

The Stormstown Traffic Inspector must inform the Trainmen of all Down trains picking up at Pont Shon Norton Storage Sidings how many wagons they have to pick up, and the Drivers in bringing their trains to a stand, must allow sufficient room clear of points for the traffic they have to pick up when joined to the train on the Main line ready to go forward. (5,599.)

Pont Shon Norton Junction.

Wagons for Messrs. Mackay & Davies, Craig-yr-hesg, and for Mr. Thos. Taylor's Quarry must be put off by Up trains on the Up line siding at Pont Shon Norton, and by Down trains on the Down sidings and not upon the Goods Yard.   (T. 85,114.)

Mackay's Quarry Siding, Craig-yr-hesg.

This siding is on the Up side of the line, but has no direct connection with it. Access to the Quarry siding is obtained from the road running parallel to the Up Main line beside Pont Shon Norton signal box.

The gradient rises about 1 in 37 from the Main line level to the quarry.

The load for an engine proceeding to the Quarry must not exceed 20 empties. On the return journey the load must be limited to 20 laden wagons.

The engine must always be at the bottom or Pontypridd end of the train, both when going to and returning from the quarry.

On the Down journey each train must stop outside the catch points at the foot of the incline to enable the guard or brakesman, whichever may be riding on the engine, to see that the points are right for the Up line siding, and may afterwards proceed if the fixed signal is at "All Right."

Before starting on the Down journey the guard and brakesman must pin down a sufficient number of brakes to ensure the safe descent of the train, and its stopping clear of the safety points at the bottom of the incline.

The guard or brakesman must be riding on the train in such a position, both in ascending and descending the incline, as to be able to apply the brakes should it be necessary to stop at any point.

Under no circumstances may any wagons be taken up to the Quarry unless they have good brakes, and guards must be careful to reject all wagons that are not in good order.

Guards must obtain consignment notes for all traffic cleared from these Quarries and deliver the notes to the goods agent or yardman at Pontypridd.   (T. 81,440.)

Cilfynydd Ground Frame.

To prevent damage to the trailing points connected with this frame through the levers being reversed before the vehicles have passed clear, guards must satisfy themselves that engines and vehicles have passed clear of these points before they alter their position.   (T. 81,252.)

Albion Colliery, Pont Shon Norton Branch.

1. The safety points at this Colliery are worked from the Cilfynydd Loop Signal Box.

2. The guard or groundman in charge of each train must see to the opening and closing of the Colliery gate.

3 A lamp showing a red light is placed upon the gate in question before sunset or during thick or foggy weather. This lamp must be trimmed and lighted at Cilfynydd Loop Signal Box, and taken and placed upon the gate by the guard in charge of one of the trains, and must be brought from the gate to the signal box by the first train leaving the Colliery after daylight. Coal must be drawn from the Colliery to the Junction.

Ynysydwr Junction, Nelson Branch.

The points at this Junction are worked by a ground frame locked by the Electric Train Staff for the Section.

Whenever an engine or train is required to be run between Nelson and Stormstown Junction it must be worked from the Nelson end, and at a time when it will be able to work to Stormstown and back without delaying the ordinary trains or cars.

Whenever a train is required to be run between Cilfynydd Loop and Dowlais Abercynon Colliery, it must be worked from the Cilfynydd end, and at a time when it can be worked to and fro without delaying the ordinary trains or cars.   (T. 94,487.)

Electric Train Staff, Nelson Station.

The Electric Train Staff Instrument at Nelson is fixed in the Booking Office. The safety points North of the platform are worked by a Ground Frame fixed near the points. The Ground Frame is unlocked by the Electric Train Staff. (5,142.)

Level Crossing, Nelson.

In order to sufficiently warn persons using this Crossing, Drivers of approaching trains must sound the engine whistle immediately after passing under the Station bridge. Drivers must also keep a sharp look-out. (5,460.)

Nelson Branch.

1. The principal gradients are :—

Cilfynydd to Ynysydwr Rise	.. .. ..	one in 103—264
" Fall	.. .. ..	" 120— 40
Ynysydwr to Fiddler's Elbow Rise	.. .. ..	" 40—100

2. The line between Stormstown Junction and Ynysydwr Junction is worked as a Siding, and is under the control of the Signalman at Stormstown Junction. Trains or engines must not travel over this Siding at a speed exceeding eight miles per hour, and the men in charge must keep a sharp look-out for hand signals.

3. Between Pont Shon Norton Junction and Albion Colliery, the practice of propelling wagons in front of the engine is forbidden ; all the wagons must be drawn with the engine in front, and in the event of the top cross-over at Albion Colliery or the siding West of the running road being occupied and the engine being unable to run around its wagons on the Colliery Siding, the train must draw into the Cilfynydd Loop Siding, and the engine must be shunted from the front to the rear of the train so as to draw the empties back on to the Pont Shon Norton section and push them into the colliery.

4. Full loads of goods must be turned off at Stormstown, and the Traffic Inspector must arrange for all such vehicles to be marshalled in readiness to be attached to the Mixed trains. See page 50 for maximum loads.

See Special instructions on page 132 for working between Ynysydwr Junction and Stormstown.

5. All passenger trains running on this Branch must have a brake compartment with hand-brake at each end, for use in case of failure of the vacuum brake or in other emergency.

Extract from TVR Appendix to Working Timetable, 1913.

Down Relief Line, Clydach Court to Pont Shon Norton.

This line is worked under the Standard Block Telegraph Regulations, which, however, may be suspended when necessary to admit two or more trains. See page 13. (4,888.)

When it is necessary for an Ynysybwl Branch train to be accepted down the Relief line under the suspended block (see page 13), the Signalman at Clydach Court must, before accepting a train under this arrangement, comply with the instructions on page 13 and inform the Signalman at Windsor Siding how many trains there are standing on the Relief line, and the latter must warn the Driver accordingly. (4,921.)

Empties for Darranddu Colliery.

Trains conveying empties for Darranddu Colliery, except when working through to the Ynysybwl Branch, must put the Darranddu empties off in Stormstown Jct., from which point they must be cleared under the instructions of the Stormstown Traffic Inspector. (5,432.)

Mynachdy Colliery, Ynysybwl Branch.

A bolt and padlock have been fixed to the points connecting this Colliery Siding with the T.V. line, also to the catch points at the lower end of the T.V. Siding. The key is kept at Ynysybwl, and must be carried, together with the Staff for the Section, by all trains picking up or putting off. (6,045.)

Stormstown Junction and Clydach Court to the end of Ynysybwl Branch.

1. The principal gradients are :—
   Above Ynysybwl Station 1 in 30, 32, and 35 falling towards Ynysybwl.
   Below   „   „   1 in 40 and 43   „   „   Stormstown.
2. The speed of goods and mineral trains on falling gradients must not exceed eight miles per hour.
   The speed of passenger trains must not exceed that shown in the Working Time Tables.
3. The loads of goods and mineral trains must be limited as shown below :—

   Up Trains.
   { Stormstown to Windsor Passing Siding 28 empty wagons, or equivalent thereto.
   { Windsor Passing Siding and Ynysybwl 28   „   „   „
   { Ynysybwl to end of Branch 20   „   „   „

   Down Trains
   { Top of Branch to Ynysybwl .. .. 25 laden   „   „   „
   { Ynysybwl to Stormstown Junction .. 40   „   „   „

4. All passenger trains running on this Branch must have a brake compartment with hand-brake at each end for use in case of failure of the vacuum brake or in other emergency. A Guard must ride in the brake compartment at each end of the train unless otherwise ordered by the Superintendent of the Line.
5. The last vehicle of every goods or mineral train between Ynysybwl and Stormstown Junction, both on the Up and Down journeys, must be a brakevan.
6. Above Ynysybwl the engine must invariably be at the Ynysybwl or lower end of the train.
7. On all sections of this branch, whenever a train is brought to a stand for shunting or other purposes, before detaching the engine, the guard must put down and secure as many brakes as may be necessary to prevent the train running away.
8. All goods and mineral brakevans working on this section must be supplied with brake sticks, sprags, and scotches for use. if necessary ; at least two of each to be supplied.
9. The points leading to the old warehouse siding act as a safety trap, and have to be held over for trains from the top end of the Branch to proceed towards Ynysybwl Station.
10. The speed of all trains while travelling from Windsor Siding to Clydach Court must not exceed *eight miles per hour*, and all trains must stop clear of the Down Branch Home Signal at Clydach Court.
11. The loads of all trains must be limited as shown below :—

    Clydach Court to Windsor Siding, 28 empty wagons or equivalent thereto for one engine.
    „   „   „   55 empty wagons or equivalent thereto for two engines.
    Windsor Siding to Clydach Court, 40 laden wagons or equivalent thereto for one engine.
    „   „   „   55 laden wagons or equivalent thereto for two engines.

    When an assistant engine is used it must be at the rear on the Up journey and in front on the Down journey.
12. Traffic for Windsor Colliery and Ynysybwl must be retained for the trains that are booked to work through to destination, and when there is no bank engine available, the load must be reduced at Clydach Court, and the train engine must after working the first part to the Colliery, return to Clydach Court for the remainder.
13. The signalman at Treforest (Barry) Junction must telephone to the Traffic Inspector at Stormstown the time of departure of all trains for Windsor Colliery and the number of wagons on, to enable arrangements to be made for a bank engine to be available.
14. The last vehicle of every goods or mineral train between Windsor Siding and Clydach Court, both on the Up and Down journeys, must be a brakevan.
15. Whenever a train is brought to a stand for shunting or other purposes, before detaching the engine the guard must put down and secure as many brakes as may be necessary to prevent the train running away.
16. All goods and mineral trains working upon this section of the line must be supplied with brake sticks sprags, and scotches for use, if necessary ; at least two of each must be supplied. (2,502)
17. All Down Mineral trains must stop at the gradient post below Windsor Siding Up Distant signal to enable the guard to apply more brakes if required. (2,526)
18. Down mineral trains from Lady Windsor Colliery must stop at Clydach Court Home signal to pick up brakes, before running out on to the Main line.
19. The guard and groundman must pick up the brakes ; and, if required by the engine driver, a few brakes nearest to the engine must be left on until the signal is lowered, and the groundman must stand by to release them.

T 69,714.

Extract from TVR Appendix to Working Timetable, 1913.

TRAINS AND STEAM MOTOR CARS

Between PONTYPRIDD & NELSON, also between PONTYPRIDD & YNYSYBWL.

YNYSYBWL SECTION.

UP.

	A.M.	A.M.	A.M.	A.M.	P.M.	P.M.	P.M.	P.M.	P.M.	P.M.		P.M.		Sats. only.	P.M.	P.M.	
Connecting Trns arr P'pridd	A.M.																
From Rhondda at ..	6 57	8 10	9 50	11 13	12 27	1 41	2 43	4 14	4 55	6 0	..	8 11	..	..	9 34		
„ Cardiff „ ..	6 59	8 35	9 44	11 10	12 31	1 42	3 29	4 27	5 11	6 27	..	8 18	..	..	10 19	..	
„ Merthyr „ ..	..	8 25	9 1	11 2	..	1 26	2 46	4 26	..	6 15	..	7 57	..	..	9 37		
„ Aberdare „ ..	..	8 25	9 1	11 2	..	1 26	2 46	4 26	5 10	6 15	..	7 57	..	..	9 37		
„ Cowbridge „ ..	..	8 19	9 4	11 1	..	1 21	2 46	4 9	..	6 17	..	7 37	..	..	9 37		
Pontypridd .. ..dep	7 20	8 40	9 55	11 27	12 35	1 56	3 38	4 35	5 23	6 30	..	8 32	..	*9 26*	10 25	..	
Clydach Court .. „	..	8 46	..	..	12 41	2 2	..	4 41	5 29	6 36	..	8 38	..	*9 32*	..	..	
Ynysybwl (New Road) „	7 30	8 51	10 5	11 37	12 46	2 7	3 48	4 46	5 34	6 41	..	8 43	..	*9 37*	10 35	..	
Robertstown .. „	7 33	8 54	10 8	11 40	12 49	2 10	3 51	4 49	5 37	6 44	..	8 46	..	*9 40*	10 38	..	
Ynysybwl .. „	7 36	8 57	10 10	11 42	12 51	2 13	3 53	4 51	5 40	6 47	..	8 49	..	*9 42*	10 40	..	
Old Ynysybwl .. arr	7 38	8 59	10 13	11 45	12 54	2 15	3 56	4 53	5 42	6 49	..	8 51	..	..	10 43	..	

DOWN.

	A.M.	A.M.	A.M.	P.M.	P.M.	P.M.	P.M.	P.M.	P.M.		P.M.		Sats. only.	P.M.	P.M.	
Old Ynysybwl.. ..dep	7 42	9 11	10 41	12 3	12 58	2 19	4 4	4 58	5 46	..	7 30	..	8 57	..	10 48	
Ynysybwl .. „	7 45	9 14	10 44	12 6	1 1	2 22	4 7	5 1	5 49	..	7 33	..	9 0	*9 53*	10 51	..
Robertstown .. „	7 48	9 17	10 47	12 9	1 4	2 25	4 10	5 4	5 52	..	7 36	..	9 3	*9 56*	10 54	..
Ynysybwl (New Road) „	7 53	9 20	10 50	12 12	1 7	2 28	4 13	5 7	5 55	..	7 39	..	9 6	*9 59*	10 57	..
Clydach Court .. „	7 57	9 24	..	..	..	2 32	..	5 11	5 59	..	7 43	..	9 10	..	..	
Pontypridd .. ..arr	8 0	9 29	10 58	12 20	1 15	2 37	4 21	5 16	6 4	..	7 48	..	9 15	*10 7*	11 5	..

Connecting Trn leave P'p'dd																
For Cardiff at ..	8 14	9 54	11 18	12 30	1 28	2 49	4 29	5 27	6 17	..	8 15	..	9 43	..	..	
„ Rhondda „ ..	8 7	9 49	11 23	12 34	1 33	3 47	4 40	5 50	6 31	..	8 3	..	9 54	*10 25*	..	
„ Aberdare „ ..	8 14	9 33	11 18	..	1 47	3 32	4 32	5 30	6 15	..	8 21	..	10 22	*10 22*	..	
„ Merthyr „ ..	8 14	9 33	11 18	..	1 47	3 32	4 32	..	6 15	..	8 21	..	10 22	*10 22*	..	
„ Cowbridge „ ..	8 30	10 0	11 21	..	1 38	3 7	5 15	..	6 38	..	8 35	..	10 0	..	..	

* Runs to and from Ynysybwl only on Saturdays.

NELSON SECTION.

UP.

		Work men.	Weds only.												
Connecting Trns arr P'pridd		A.M.	A.M.	A.M.	A.M.	A.M.	P.M.			P.M.	P.M.		P.M.		
From Rhondda at ..	..	..	6 57	*9 50*	11 13	1 30	..		..	1 41	4 55	..	8 11	..	
„ Cardiff „ ..	..	*5 31*	6 59	*9 44*	11 10	1 29	..		..	1 42	5 11	..	8 18	..	
„ Cowbridge „ ..	..	..	..	*9 4*	11 1	1 21	..		..	..	4 9	..	7 37	..	
Pontypridd .. ..dep	..	*5 48*	7 5	*10 15*	11 25	1 34	..		2 40	5 18	..	8 23	..	
Berw Road .. „	..	..	7 8	*10 18*	11 28	1 37	..	Workmen and ordinary Passengers.	2 43	5 21	..	8 26	..	
Cilfynydd .. „	..	*5 55*	7 13	*10 23*	11 33	1 42	..		2 48	5 26	..	8 31	..	
Travellers Rest .. „	..	6 2	7 18	*10 28*	11 39	1 48	..		2 53	5 32	..	8 37	..	
Llanfabon Rd. Halt .. „	..	6 7	7 23	*10 33*	11 46	1 55	..		2 58	5 39	..	8 44	..	
Nelson .. .. ..arr	..	6 9	7 25	*10 35*	11 48	1 57	..		3 0	5 41	..	8 46	..	

DOWN.

		Work men.	Weds only.										
		A.M.	A.M.	A M	P.M.	P.M.			P.M.		P.M.		P.M.
Nelson .. .. ..dep	..	6 22	7 40	*10 50*	12 58	2 5	..	..	4 0	..	5 50	..	9 12
Llanfabon Rd. Halt .. „	..	6 24	7 42	*10 52*	1 0	2 7	..	..	4 2	..	5 52	..	9 14
Travellers' Rest .. „	..	6 29	7 47	*10 58*	1 7	2 14	..	..	4 7	..	5 59	..	9 21
Cilfynydd .. „	..	6 37	7 52	*11 3*	1 12	2 19	..	..	4 12	..	6 4	..	9 26
Berw Road .. „	..	..	7 57	*11 8*	1 17	2 24	..	..	4 17	..	6 9	..	9 31
Pontypridd .. ..arr	..	6 43	7 59	*11 10*	1 19	2 26	..	..	4 19	..	6 11	..	9 33

Connecting Trs leave P'p'dd													
For Rhondda at ..	..	7 4	8 7	*11 23*	1 33	3 47	..	..	4 40	..	6 31	..	9 54
„ Cardiff „ ..	..	6 59	8 14	*11 18*	1 28	2 49	..	..	4 29	..	6 17	..	9 43
„ Cowbridge „ ..	..	..	8 30	*11 21*	1 38	3 7	..	..	5 15	..	6 38	..	10 0

TVR public timetable, 5th December, 1921.

towards the cost of its maintenance. In 1908 the GWR had suggested that this connection should be removed, but it had been left in place in view of its possible use by the proposed motor car service. In 1910 it was agreed to take out the connection on the understanding that it would be reinstated by the GWR whenever the TVR might require it. As part of major alterations at Llancaiach, carried out at this time, the old GWR passenger station was swept away and replaced by a commodious new station, known as 'Nelson and Llancaiach', just beyond Taff Bargoed Junction. The new station also included extensive goods facilities, and from 5th August, 1912 the GWR ceased to use the TVR goods station at Nelson and transferred its goods traffic to the new station. This resulted in there being no regular traffic over the Llancaiach Junction.

The Great War brought pressures for reductions in services and economies in operation. Timetables were progressively reduced and train mileage curtailed. As the war entered a more determined phase, demands were made for even more drastic savings. On 19th December, 1916 the TVR Board considered a letter from the wartime Railway Executive Committee stating that the Board of Trade was reviewing the question of closing certain branch lines to enable the permanent way materials to be released for the war effort. The TVR was asked to nominate any lightly used lines which might be sacrificed to this end. In response, the company identified a number of sections that could be closed, including those from Mynachdy Colliery to the end of the Ynysybwl Branch and from Stormstown Junction to Windsor Passing Siding. Such drastic action proved unnecessary, however, as on 30th January, 1917, the TVR Board was informed that the Railway Executive Committee did not, for the time being, contemplate making use of permanent way materials from the sections in question.

Wartime conditions also brought dramatic increases in certain traffic flows, in particular the transport of coal for the Navy. In pre-war days most of this coal had been moved by coastal shipping, but during the war a vast traffic developed between South Wales and Scotland for transfer to the Northern Fleet. Congestion became a serious problem at Quaker's Yard, where traffic was exchanged between the TVR and GWR. However, physical conditions at this junction prevented any significant increase in siding capacity. In order to overcome this problem, the TVR Traffic Committee agreed, on 29th January, 1918, to a proposal to provide extra accommodation at Stormstown Junction. This decision was subsequently confirmed by the War Office, but the improvements were not completed until after the signing of the Armistice in November 1918. Alternative routes were also developed to ease the pressure on established ones. On 27th March, 1918 it was reported that arrangements had been made to work part of the traffic for the north, previously conveyed via Quaker's Yard, by way of the Alexandra (Newport & South Wales) Dock & Railway (ex-PC&NR) line, Penrhos and Aber Junctions, and Ystrad Mynach.

Following the return of peace consideration was given to the future of the national railway network, weakened as a result of the pressures and shortages of the war years. The various independent companies of South Wales were amalgamated with the GWR under the Railway Act of 19th August, 1921, and on 25th March, 1922, (effective from 1st January, 1922) the TVR, as a 'Constituent' company, became part of the enlarged GWR.

The vast island platform at Pontypridd, viewed from above on 12th June, 1956.   *S. Rickard*

Class '54XX' 0-6-0PT No. 5421 and auto-trailer at Pontypridd on the last day of the Ynysybwl service, 26th July, 1952.   *R.C. Riley*

Chapter Seven

Along the Lines

This description of the Nelson and Ynysybwl branches takes the form of a tour of the lines, as they were in the final days of the TVR. Pontypridd, at the hub of the system, was the logical starting point for such a tour. In 1922 services radiated from the station in all directions, in addition to the main line trains which passed through between Cardiff and Merthyr. The Nelson and Ynysybwl trains left from bays at the Merthyr end of the station, the former usually from the inset bay (Platform 5) adjoining the down main line, and the latter from one of the short motor bays (Platform 4), cut into the northern extremity of the vast island platform. All distances given are taken from the Cardiff Docks terminus of the TVR.

Departing the station, trains for the two branches took the Merthyr line at Pontypridd Junction, before crossing the River Rhondda by means of a stone arched viaduct. Originally single track with one large and three small semi-circular arches, it was widened in 1847, but with five arches of equal span on the new portion, because of doubts concerning the stability of the original single large arch.

Beyond the viaduct, the line curved past Pontypridd goods station, opened in 1888, when it replaced the original goods yard, south of the passenger station. Opposite the goods station the North Curve, which provided a direct link from the Rhondda branch, joined the main line at Pontypridd Northern Junction. From this junction to Pont Shon Norton and Clydach Court Junctions there were three lines of rails - up main, down main and down relief.

When brought into use in 1884, Pont Shon Norton Junction (13 m. 56 ch.) was a simple affair on a double track section of the main line about a mile north of the limits of the junctions at Pontypridd. By 1922, however, it had become, to all intents and purposes, part of the great complex of railway lines which sprawled along the valleys out of Pontypridd. As well as being the junction for the branch to Nelson, Pont Shon Norton Junction was also the point at which a lengthy private siding left the main line. Opened in 1886, this line served the Graig-yr-Hesg quarry, about ¾ mile to the north of the junction. In addition, there was also a traffic siding, just to the north of the junction, served off the down relief line.

The Nelson Branch

Immediately after leaving Pont Shon Norton Junction, the Nelson train would have arrived at Berw Road Platform (13 m. 75 ch.), a typical TVR structure, only 40 ft long, without any form of shelter and approached by a ramp from Berw Road (the main road from Pontypridd to Ynysybwl). Just beyond the platform, the line crossed Berw Road by means of a plate girder bridge, and then the River Taff by an impressive viaduct, consisting of three lattice girder spans resting on

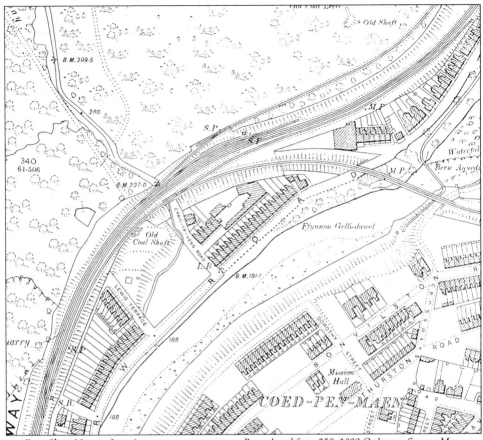

Pont Shon Norton Junction.   *Reproduced from 25", 1898 Ordnance Survey Map*

Berw Road (by then) Halt, looking towards Merthyr, on 25th May, 1959.   *M. Hale*

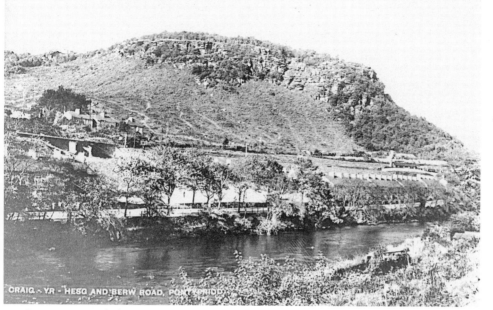

Graig-y-Hesg, with the TVR main line and Pont Shon Norton branch crossing the centre of the picture, and Berw Road Platform on the extreme right.   *Pontypridd Library*

Berw Road Halt, looking towards Pont Shon Norton Junction.   *C.W. Harris*

The viaduct over the River Taff on the Pont Shon Norton branch, proudly proclaiming its ownership and completion date.   *Ian Pope Collection*

The viaduct carrrying the Pont Shon Norton branch over the River Taff, near Berw Road, in the early years of this century.   *Pontypridd Library*

stone piers and abutments, with the parapets above the piers proudly proclaiming the date of the viaduct's completion (1885) and the railway company's initials in bold raised figures.

Once across the viaduct, the line curved past the remains of Coedpenmaen station (14 m. 11 ch.). This originally had consisted of a single platform with the standard type of station building used for stations between Pontypridd and Nelson. These buildings were of brick construction, with timber front elevation and a full length canopy providing shelter for intending passengers.

By 1922 the built-up area extended almost all the way along the main road from Pontypridd to Cilfynydd. After leaving Coedpenmaen, however, the railway passed at a lower level and retained much of its earlier rural character. Midway between Coedpenmaen and Cilfynydd was a loop siding (14 m. 32 ch.) serving a quarry belonging to Thomas Taylor of Pontypridd. The siding connections were controlled by two ground frames and the whole had been approved by the Traffic Committee on 19th October, 1897, at an estimated cost of £272.

After Taylor's Siding the line continued along the lower level of the hillside to Cilfynydd, where, in its original form, the Pont Shon Norton branch had terminated in an end-on junction with the Albion Colliery sidings. The colliery itself was a substantial affair with a siding capacity of 725 wagons in 1897, when the colliery company owned a total of 600 wagons. When the Cilfynydd Loop was constructed, the line had to snake past the western limits of the colliery, before returning to the eastern slopes of the Taff Valley. A loop was installed at the colliery junction, at which two goods or mineral trains or one passenger and one goods or mineral train could pass. The southern end of this loop (14 m. 67 ch.) was controlled by a signal box, containing 12 levers, of which all but one were in use, whilst the northern end of the loop (15 m. 4 ch.) was worked by a ground frame, unlocked by the electric train staff for the section between Cilfynydd and Nelson.

Cilfynydd passenger station (15 m. 13 ch.) was situated on the single track section beyond the passing loop. Two goods sidings ran from the loop to the small yard at the rear of the passenger platform. Road access to the goods yard and the passenger station was via a steeply graded ramp from the road which bridged the railway immediately north of the station. Pedestrians also had the use of a lengthy footbridge which crossed the colliery sidings to the south of the station to reach the centre of the village. Despite this feature, however, the station was poorly sited for the majority of the village, being cut off from it by the colliery and its extensive sidings. The tramway, on the other hand, ran along the main street, effectively serving the linear settlement throughout its length.

After passing under the overbridge to the north of the station the line was joined by an upper connection (15 m. 40 ch.) from the Albion Colliery. From this point to Ynysydwr Junction, the branch passed through an unspoilt rural area, keeping company with the Glamorganshire Canal and the former turnpike road, both of which pursued their routes at higher levels up the valley side. At 15 m. 76 ch. the line to the Dowlais-Cardiff Colliery left the main branch, by means of a simple facing connection, controlled by a two-lever ground frame,

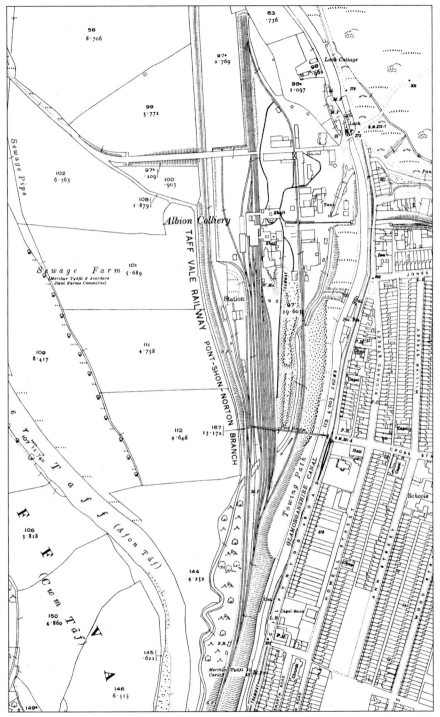

Cilfynydd station and Albion Colliery.   *Reproduced from 25", 1915 Ordnance Survey Map*

Cilfynydd station provides the unintentional backdrop to this 1930s view.

T.J. McCarthy Collection

Albion Colliery, Cilfynydd, with TVR 'Loco' coal wagons in the sidings alongside the usual 'Albion' wagons.

J.A. Peden Collection

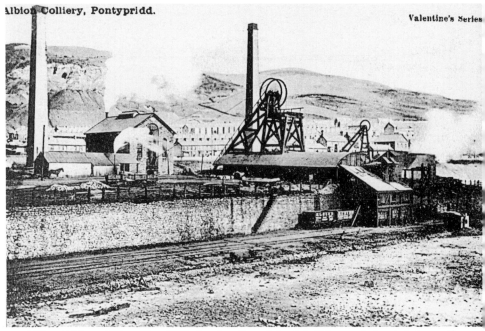

Albion Colliery, Cilfynydd *c.* 1900, showing the substantial difference in levels between the colliery itself and the railway sidings. *Welsh Industrial & Maritime Museum*

Albion Colliery, Cilfynydd *c.* 1910, viewed from the village. *Welsh Industrial Maritime Museum*

Albion Colliery, Cilfynydd, Pontypridd

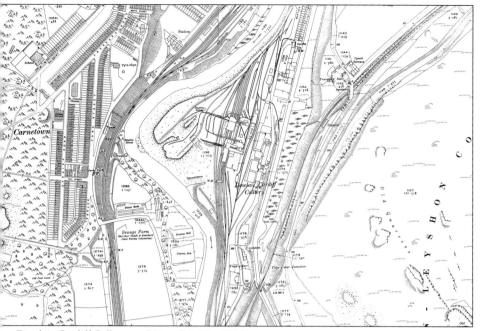

Dowlais-Cardiff Colliery and Travellers' Rest Halt.

Reproduced from the 25″, 1919 Ordnance Survey Map

Dowlais-Cardiff Colliery, Abercynon, with the station building at Travellers' Rest in the foreground.
Welsh Industrial & Maritime Museum

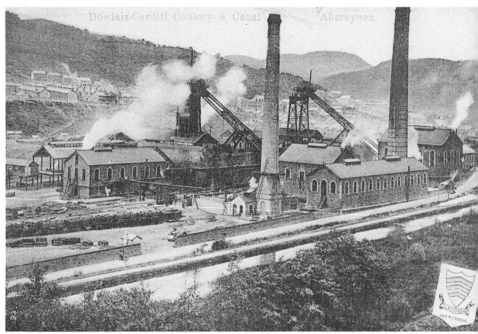

Dowlais-Cardiff Colliery, looking towards Merthyr, with the Glamorganshire Canal in the foreground. *Ian Pope Collection*

A former TVR class '04' 0-6-2T, as rebuilt by the GWR, crosses the three-arched bridge at Llanfabon Road, on the Nelson branch, shortly before the withdrawal of the passenger service. *E. Evans Collection*

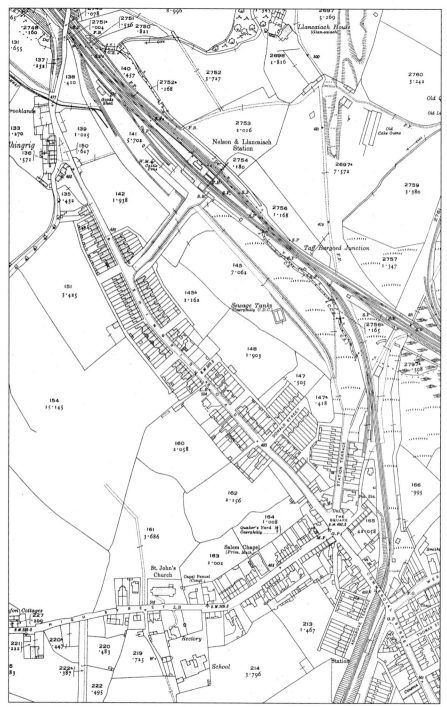

The TVR station at Nelson, together with Nelson and Llancaiach (GWR) station.
Reproduced from the 25″, 1915 Ordnance Survey Map

Above: Nelson station in TVR days, looking towards Llancaiach Junction, showing the 'unsightly' hoarding alongside the approach ramp, which was objected to by the local Chamber of Trade.

Lens of Sutton

Right: Nelson station after the track had been lifted from a point just beyond the Pontypridd end of the platform. *E. Evans Collection*

The remaining section of the Nelson branch, retained as sidings from Llancaiach Junction, on 4th September, 1957. *M. Hale*

unlocked by the key from the electric train staff for the Cilfynydd to Nelson section. The colliery line passed under a plate girder bridge, built wide enough for double track, which carried the line from Stormstown Junction to Ynysydwr Junction, before joining the original Dowlais-Cardiff Colliery siding.

Beyond this junction the line curved and climbed to Ynysydwr Junction (16 m. 19 ch.), where the Cilfynydd Loop joined the Nelson Branch proper. When opened in 1900, this simple junction was controlled by a signal box, but this saw little use and was closed in 1903, being replaced by a ground frame, unlocked by the electric train staff. Travellers' Rest station (16 m. 36 ch.), just beyond the junction, was a single platform affair, originally with the standard type of station building. The station had been opened to serve Dowlais-Cardiff Colliery, and there was little in the way of settlement nearby, save for the public house of the same name and Cynon Terrace.

Thus far, the gradients had been relatively easy, but from Ynysydwr Junction the line climbed at 1 in 40 towards Fidler's Elbow. This was, of course, small beer compared with the earlier rope-worked incline, which could be seen alongside making its ascent out of the valley to reach its windy ledge high up on the hillside. The old and new routes came together at St Cynon's Church, but parted company just beyond at Fidler's Elbow, where the original line passed through a very sharp curve, while the later line followed an easier radius, cut into the hillside. The two routes merged just beyond Fidler's Elbow and from this point the line followed the route of the original Llancaiach branch, opened in 1841. It was also the place where the branch finally left the Taff Valley to follow the side valley of the Nant Mafon, to Abernant House. Midway between Fidler's Elbow and Abernant House a siding had been installed in 1903 to serve Whitehall Quarry. This siding, in the form of a loop controlled by two ground frames, was the subject of a favourable inspection report, dated 19th November, 1903, by Colonel Druitt for the Board of Trade, but proved rather short-lived, having gone by 1913.

From the site of the quarry siding the line passed along an embankment through rolling countryside to Llanfabon Road Platform (18 m. 11 ch.). This Platform was situated on the embankment and was approached by means of a ramp from the adjoining road. It served the small community of Tai'r Heol, together with Abernant House and the Railway Inn. On 16th June, 1908, following an application from Nelson Chamber of Trade, the Traffic Committee agreed to provide a shelter at Llanfabon Road Platform, at an estimated cost of £18. Just beyond the end of the platform, the line crossed Llanfabon Road by means of a triple-arched stone bridge, which originally had timber spans. This had been the point at which Sir Christopher Smith's Tramroad had crossed from the north side to the south side of the railway, along the route later taken by the road from St Cynon's Church to Nelson.

East of Llanfabon Road Platform, just beyond Tai-machine - the old tramroad weighbridge house, was another loop siding, controlled by two ground frames. This siding had been installed under a private siding agreement between the TVR and the Berthgron Quarry Co., dated 24th June, 1907. The quarry itself was connected to the siding by means of a tramway across the intervening fields. The siding agreement was transferred to W.E. Lewis & Sons Ltd on 5th

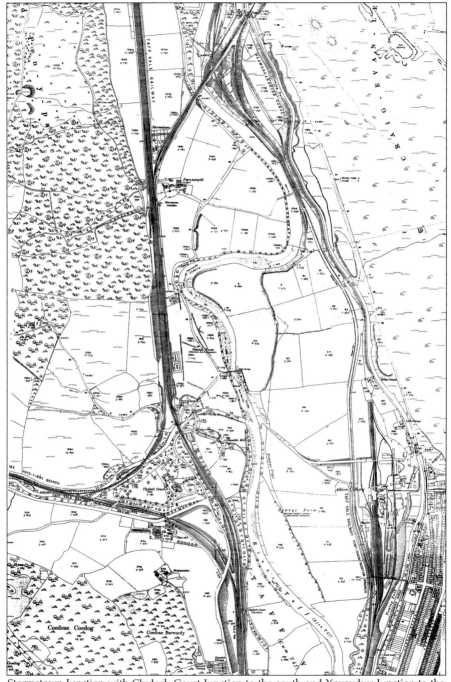

Stormstown Junction with Clydach Court Junction to the south and Ynysydwr Junction to the north-east. The line running almost due north is for Abercynon, whilst that running to the south-east is to Pont Shon Norton Junction via Cilfynydd (the Nelson branch).

Reproduced from the 25″, 1919 Ordnance Survey Map

December, 1919 and to E. Lewis & Sons Ltd on 5th July, 1929, but in January 1930 it was reported that the siding had been removed.

From Berthgron Quarry Siding the line curved to the north, before entering a cutting and running into Nelson station (18 m. 65 ch.), the terminus for the passenger train service. The facilities here were extremely simple, with the standard pattern station building on a single platform, which was approached by a ramp from Commercial Street. Dynevor Terrace ran parallel with the railway and alongside the station. For many years this frontage was dominated by a large advertising hoarding, owned by the railway company. In January 1907 its Traffic Committee rejected a request from Nelson Chamber of Trade, seeking the removal of this 'unsightly' structure.

While motor cars and auto-trains went no further than the passenger station, any ordinary trains continued under the bridge carrying Commercial Street, to the loop for the engine to run round. The line had been fully signalled at this point in 1878, including the abortive east curve, but this had gone by 1898. However, in conjunction with the introduction of the passenger service in 1900 a new signal box was provided, together with the necessary signals, at a cost of £675. This proved to be something of an extravagance and on 9th July, 1907 the Traffic Committee agreed to remove the box and signals and to substitute a ground frame and relocate the electric train staff equipment to the booking office. The cost of these alterations was put at £40, but they were expected to produce a saving of £31 4s. p.a. in wages alone.

The goods yard was situated alongside the loop and comprised two short sidings and a small goods shed. A tramway had run from the goods yard to Mathias Brothers' Park Quarry and Richard Griffith's Park Colliery, both to the north-west of Nelson, but by 1915 this had been diverted to the new GWR station of Nelson & Llancaiach. Beyond the yard the line made a trailing connection with the GWR at Llancaiach Junction (19 m. 12 ch.). Around the line, at this point, traces could be discerned of the remains of early tramroads, colliery sidings and the eastern curve, records of the long and complex history of the Nelson branch.

The line from Pont Shon Norton Junction to Nelson was worked on the electric train staff system and divided into two sections: Pont Shon Norton Junction to Cilfynydd (red staff in TVR days) and Cilfynydd to Nelson (blue staff).

The Ynysybwl Branch

Just over ¼ mile north of Pont Shon North Junction, the TVR main line passed under a bridge carrying Berw Road, the main road between Pontypridd and Ynysybwl. Immediately to the south of this bridge was the original site of Berw Road Platform. Platforms were provided on each side of the main line, linked by ramps to the main road. The site was about 300 yards north of the replacement platform on the Pont Shon Norton branch and was situated on the edge of the built-up area.

The Clydach Court Loop left the main line at Clydach Court Junction (14 m.

Class '56XX' 0-6-2T No. 5644 passes Clydach Court Junction on an up freight train on 5th November, 1958. *S. Rickard*

Clydach Court Halt retained all its TVR features, including the fenced enclosure in which passengers were restrained pending the arrival of the motor car or auto-train. *R.C. Riley*

A distant view of Stormstown Junction on 2nd June, 1965, with the Ynysybwl line on the left of the picture running parallel with the ex-TVR main line.　　　　　*M. Hale*

Stormstown Junction signal box.　　　　　*David Nicholas*

Class '56XX' 0-6-2T No. 6692 at Windsor Passing Siding signal box, on 25th August, 1959.
M. Hale

The remains of Ynysybwl (New Road) Halt on 25th May, 1959, with the private siding going off to Lady Windsor Colliery on the left of the picture.
M. Hale

Lady Windsor Colliery, looking away from the village, *c.* 1910.   *Author's Collection*

Lady Windsor Colliery *c.* 1910, looking towards Ynysybwl station.   *Ian Pope Collection*

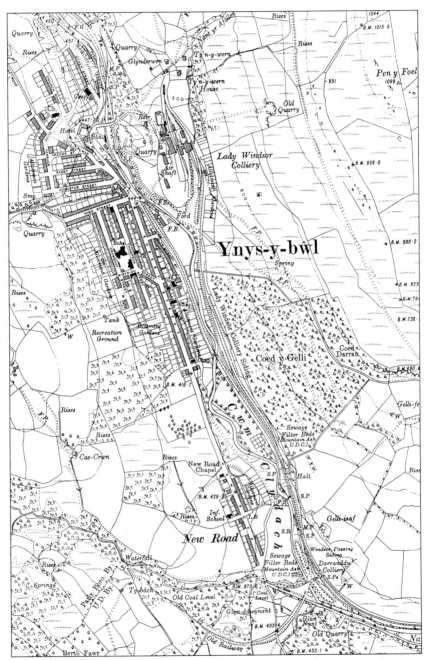

The Ynysybwl branch from Windsor Passing Siding in the south to Ynysybwl station, including Lady Windsor Colliery.   *Reproduced from the 6", 1921 Ordnance Survey Map*

61 ch.), about a mile north of Pont Shon Norton Junction. Two sidings were provided on the western side of the main line, with connections from the branch and the main line. The points on the branch were set so that these sidings acted as a trap, in the event of wild runs from the Ynysybwl line. The TVR signal box was situated on the west side of the main line, directly opposite the junction itself. This box was destroyed by fire on 18th April, 1940, and was replaced by a standard GWR structure, opened later that year, in the vee between the branch and the main line.

Just beyond the junction the branch passed under a substantial plate girder bridge, built wide enough for double track, with massive stone abutments. Seventeen chains from the junction the first motor car platform was reached. Clydach Court Platform (14 m. 78 ch.) was situated on a gradient of 1 in 47, which presented a serious problem for cars calling at the platform. In later years few services called at Clydach Court as this operating handicap was accompanied by a distinct lack of passenger traffic.

At mile post 15½ the Clydach Court Loop met the original line from Stormstown Junction and from there the two lines ran alongside each other to Windsor Passing Siding (16 m. 3 ch.). As well as enabling trains to cross or be overtaken (the latter being a positive feature of the changes insisted upon by the Board of Trade in 1889), Windsor Passing Siding was also the junction for some important colliery sidings. By 1889 the Great Western Colliery had been connected to the then down line at the passing loop. This line curved sharply away from the Ynysybwl branch to reach the colliery. On 6th October, 1891 a private siding agreement was entered into with the Darranddu Colliery Co. for another connection off this line. The two undertakings appear to have been merged by 1894 when only Darranddu Colliery was listed, this being the property of Thomas Taylor of Pontypridd. The private siding agreement was terminated on 30th June, 1928.

The other colliery which was served from Windsor Passing Siding was an altogether more substantial affair, as indicated by its siding capacity of 400 wagons in 1895. Lady Windsor Colliery was reached by a private siding, about ½ mile long and connected to the goods loop at Windsor Passing Siding. The various connections and signals at the junction were controlled by a standard TVR timber-built signal box, situated at the mid point on the passing loop. Immediately beyond the loop was Ynysybwl (New Road) Platform, reached from the settlement to the west of the river by means of a lengthy footpath and footbridge over the river.

Up to this point the railway had kept close company with the River Clydach and the main road, both of which were to the south of the line. Shortly after leaving Windsor Passing Siding, the branch crossed the river by means of a steel girder bridge, to run between it and the main road as far as Ynysybwl station. The private siding to Lady Windsor Colliery, on the other hand, stuck to the opposite bank of the river. From the river bridge the 'main line' ran along the edge of the built-up area of Robertstown and Ynysybwl, which in 1922 extended for about 2 miles along the floor and western side of the valley.

Robertstown Platform (16 m. 42 ch.) served the lower part of the urban area and was situated at the junction of Glyn-mynach Street and Glyn Street. The

A TVR motor car approaches Robertstown Platform on the Ynysybwl branch, *c.* 1905.
Welsh Industrial and Maritime Museum

The site of Robertstown Halt on the Ynysybwl branch on 25th May, 1959, with the TVR distant still in place, albeit fixed at caution. *M. Hale*

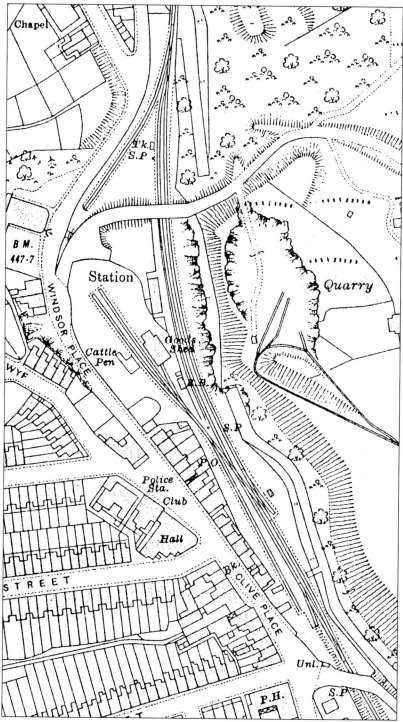

Ynysybwl station.

Reproduced from the 25″, 1915 Ordnance Survey Map

Ynysybwl station, in the late evening of its existence, but very little altered since the withdrawal of the passenger service, 25th May, 1959. *M. Hale*

Class '54XX' 0-6-0PT No. 5421 and auto-trailer at Ynysybwl on the last day of service, 26th July, 1952. *R.C. Riley*

'shelter' provided at the platform consisted of a corrugated iron pitched roof supported by six posts, the whole covering the fenced enclosure. The platform was only 600 yards from Ynysybwl station (16 m. 67 ch.), a fact emphasised by the presence of the Ynysybwl up distant signal opposite the platform.

The approach to Ynysybwl station was in cutting, the line passing under a skew bridge carrying Gelli Road, just before the station throat. The station itself was neat and compact, the buildings displaying an architectural unity not always found in TVR stations in the coalfield valleys. The passenger facilities were contained in a single storey stone building, with a gabled slated roof and yellow brick detailing. Nearby on the single platform was a timber-built signal box, situated at a point where visibility on the curve through the station was at a maximum. To the rear of the passenger station was the small goods yard comprising two parallel sidings, one of which served a stone-built goods shed and the other a cattle pen, installed following an application by local butchers in April 1904. There was also a very short spur off the goods shed siding, reputedly used for supplying coal for the signal box.

The line passed through Ynysybwl station on a gradient of 1 in 51. As a result special precautions were necessary, as explained in some detail by the working instructions issued at the opening of the line to passengers in 1890:

> A double line has been laid at this station for a distance of 390 yards, commencing at a point 145 yards south of the signal cabin, with a pair of facing points fitted with a facing point lock, and terminating with a pair of points 245 yards north of the signal cabin. The line on the left hand side approaching the station from Stormstown is the platform line for arrival and departures of all passenger trains, and all Down mineral trains proceeding beyond the station.
>
> The line on the right hand side is the Up mineral line. Sidings have been laid down for the warehouse. A connection has been laid just below the platform from the Up line to these sidings, and a compound [i.e. single slip] which forms a cross-over road between the platform line and Up line.
>
> As the passenger trains proceeding towards Stormstown go through this compound in order to avoid passing over the runaway siding in the Down main line (and which is placed to catch vehicles should they run back from the platform), the points at the top end of this compound have been fitted with a facing point lock. The points at the top end of the double line have also been fitted with a facing point lock.
>
> A facing trap, fitted with a facing point lock, has been laid in the Up line, opposite the top end of the compound, to protect Up passenger trains when travelling through the cross-over road. A self-acting back trap has been fixed in the Down platform line to catch vehicles should they run back from the platform. Under no consideration should this trap be left in other than the normal position as a runaway siding.

It will be recalled that in 1900, on the opening of the Clydach Court Loop, the 'up' and 'down' appellations on the Ynysybwl branch were reversed, bringing it into line with the rest of the TVR system, where 'up' was 'up the valley' and 'down' was 'down to Cardiff'.

By 1926 the complicated layout described at Ynysybwl station had been simplified, with the short up and down double line section being abolished. As a result, all passenger workings were confined to the up and down through line, with the loop line retained for goods and mineral traffic only.

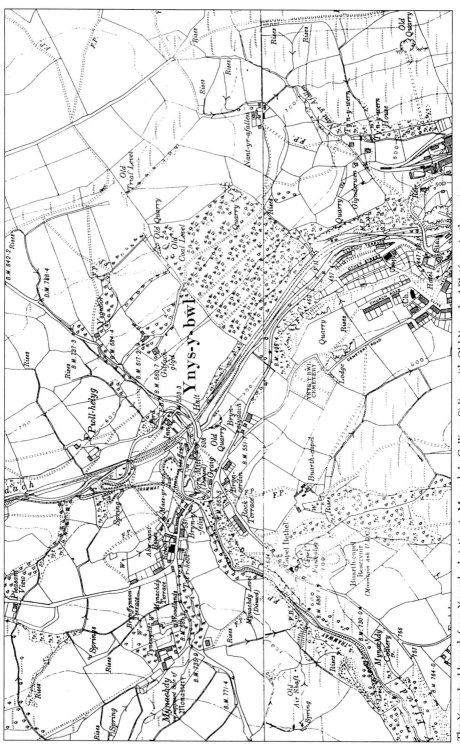

The Ynysybwl branch from Ynysybwl station to Mynachdy Colliery Siding with Old Ynysybwl Platform in the centre.

Reproduced from the 6" 1921 Ordnance Survey Map

At the north end of the station platform the line passed under an overbridge carrying the road to Lady Windsor Colliery. Beyond this bridge a short siding ran back alongside the main road. Prior to the introduction of the motor car service in 1904 this siding had been used to stable the carriages used for the passenger service on the branch. The instructions issued by the TVR on the opening of the line to passengers in 1890 mention a carriage shed, but no other reference has been found and the existence of such a shed cannot, therefore, be confirmed. Situated between the carriage siding and the running line was a water tank, believed to have been one of the requirements of the Locomotive Superintendent authorised by the Locomotive Committee on 9th January, 1890. Just beyond the upper end of the station loop, the branch crossed the River Clydach again, and shortly after this a siding went off to serve a quarry on the eastern side of the line. A siding had existed here in the early days of the railway, but had been taken up in 1895. On 10th October, 1913 the Traffic Committee accepted an application from Mr T. Jones for a siding to the quarry, which was being reactivated. The private siding agreement was dated 27th December, 1913, and the completed siding was reported on by Colonel Druitt for the Board of Trade on 21st April, 1914. The siding connection, which was facing to up trains, was controlled by a two-lever ground frame, unlocked by the train staff for the Ynysybwl-Llanwonno section. The siding agreement was terminated in December 1927.

From here the line climbed at 1 in 50 to Old Ynysybwl Platform (17 m. 35 ch.) and in so doing made the transition from the busy mining village of 'New' Ynysybwl to a largely pre-industrial rural scene. Old Ynysybwl retained much of the character of a small rural settlement and the platform itself had a certain rustic charm. It was a favourite spot, in the days of the motor car service, for crews to pose for photographs in front of their charges, and was also a popular destination for Sunday School and other treats.

Just before Old Ynysybwl Platform was a mileage siding, known as 'Old Warehouse Siding'. There has been some confusion as to the proper names of the mileage sidings above Ynysybwl station, with the Ordnance Survey referring to Cwm Siding (on the road to Mountain Ash) as 'Old Warehouse Siding'. However, TVR records clearly distinguish between the two sidings, with the Appendix to the Working Timetable noting that 'The points leading to the old warehouse siding act as a safety trap, and have to be held over for trains from the top end of the Branch to proceed towards Ynysybwl Station'. This was not the case at Cwm Siding, where the points were facing to trains proceeding up the valley. Old Warehouse Siding was controlled by a ground frame, and there was also another just above the platform itself to protect the passenger line. On 12th January, 1914 the Traffic Committee agreed to provide ground frames at other sidings above Old Ynysybwl, for additional protection, at an estimated cost of £200.

Just beyond Old Ynysybwl Platform the line passed under an overbridge, built to single track width only, with stone abutments and a timber top. Almost immediately the line crossed the first of four bridges over the river within a distance of only half-a-mile. It then passed through a cutting and over the second river bridge to the junction with Mynachdy Colliery siding (17 m. 47

Time for a chat at Old Ynysybwl Halt, in its rebuilt form, with class '64XX' 0-6-0PT No. 6411 and ex-GWR vertical sided auto-car, 11th September, 1951. *H.C. Casserley*

An attentive stare, at Old Ynysybwl Halt on 25th May, 1946, with a class '54XX' 0-6-0PT and ex-Rhymney Railway auto-trailer. *I.L. Wright*

ch.). A level had been worked at Mynachdy before the railway arrived and the colliery itself was connected to the railway at its opening. In 1891 it was the property of Randell & Co., but was listed in TVR records as 'not working' in 1895, with the siding being lifted in the following year. In January 1901 the Traffic Committee approved an application for a siding to serve Mynachdy Colliery, the private siding agreement with the Mynachdy Colliery Co. Ltd being dated 24th March, 1902. An upper junction (17 m. 67 ch.), creating a loop siding to serve the colliery screens, was provided under a further private siding agreement, dated 7th November, 1913. A tramway connected the screens to the pit head itself.

In 1922 the layout at this place comprised a loop siding on the branch itself, from which two sidings went off to the colliery screens, merging to one to rejoin the branch at the upper junction, the whole being controlled by three ground frames. In TVR days all goods and mineral trains were propelled up the branch from Ynysybwl station, to guard against breakaways on the steep gradients, but in later years such trains were hauled to Mynachdy, where the locomotive ran round its train before propelling it to the end of the branch. The private siding agreement with the Mynachdy Colliery (1903) Co. Ltd was terminated on 15th March, 1933, but on 2nd October of that year a fresh agreement was entered into with Messrs J. & W. Wall, but for the lower junction only. This agreement was terminated on 1st October, 1942.

A few yards beyond the Mynyachdy Colliery Siding upper junction were the remains of a loop siding, which had served Black Grove Colliery. The colliery itself, about ½ mile to the north-east, had been connected to the siding by means of a steeply graded tramway. Black Grove Colliery, with its private siding agreement dating from 3rd June, 1884, was a small-scale affair, with siding accommodation for only 47 wagons. It was listed by the TVR as 'not working' between 1895 and 1898, and had gone by 1903.

The upper section of the Ynysybwl branch passed through sparsely populated country, with the valley floor being extensively wooded. Gradients stiffened after Mynachdy to 1 in 30, as the line rose to its terminus, near Llanwonno. After running almost straight for about a mile, the line curved to Cwm (or Cwm Clydach) Siding (18 m. 44 ch.), at the point where the Mountain Ash road crossed the railway. Cwm Siding comprised a single siding serving a loading platform, with a head shunt off this siding. It served a scattered agricultural community, but on at least two occasions it acted as an important railhead for major construction projects. In 1902 Thomas Taylor made use of it in connection with his contract for building Perthgelyn Reservoir, about ½ mile to the north-east along the Mountain Ash road, for Mountain Ash Urban District Council.

Taylor had toyed with the idea of rearranging the sidings to cater for his traffic, but, at the suggestion of the TVR, had opted for a cheaper solution, under an agreement dated 30th December, 1901. Under this agreement, Taylor was allowed to unload his wagons on the running line, for which catch points were installed, at his expense, this arrangement being brought into use on 6th January, 1902. A timber loading stage was erected and construction materials were taken to the contract site by means of a tramway across the mountain fields.

The rural idyll at Cwm Clydach Siding in the 1920s. The running line is on the left of the picture, with the siding to the loading bank on the right. *Ian Pope Collection*

The loading platform at Cwm Clydach after the track had been lifted, looking towards Llanwonno in 1943. *I.L. Wright*

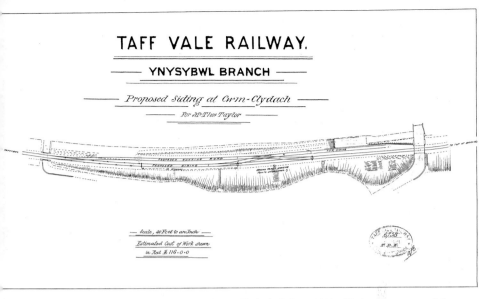

TAFF VALE RAILWAY.

—— YNYSYBWL BRANCH ——

—— Proposed Siding at Cwm-Clydach ——

—— For Mr Thos Taylor ——

— Scale, 40 Feet to an Inch —

Estimated Cost of Work shown
in Red £ 116 · 0 · 0

TVR plan of proposed re-arrangement at Cwm Clydach Siding, 1901. Under this proposal the running line would have been diverted to join the siding headshunt, whilst the siding connection would have been reversed to allow the installation of a siding to serve Thomas Taylor's unloading platform. This proved too expensive for Taylor, who was content to leave his wagons on the running line, with TVR approval.

TVR drawing showing land at the terminus of the Ynysybwl branch applied for by Mr T.W. Smith, July 1907.

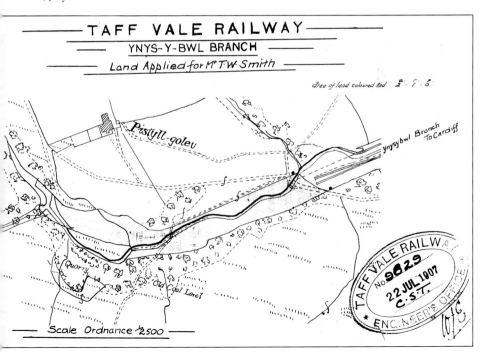

—— TAFF VALE RAILWAY ——

—— YNYS-Y-BWL BRANCH ——

—— Land Applied for Mr T.W. Smith ——

Area of land coloured Red 2 . 7 . 6

Pistyll-goleu

Ynysybwl Branch To Cardiff

Quarry

Old Coal Level

—— Scale Ordnance 1/2500 ——

In 1922 the Powell Duffryn Steam Coal Co. used Cwm Siding in connection with the provision of an overhead electricity transmission line from Middle Duffryn in the Aberdare Valley to Llantrisant. Construction materials were unloaded at the siding, it being necessary to remove the gate and post at the entrance to the yard, to enable Powell Duffryn's lorries to enter and leave. On 24th March, 1908 the Traffic Committee accepted an application from Mr J. Lewis for a temporary siding, near Cwm Siding, for loading timber, but it is not known if this was provided.

From Cwm Siding the branch curved through a broad arc, the final section of the line running in a south-westerly direction, and crossing the River Clydach at three points in the last ¼ mile. Near the terminus there was evidence of early mining activity, which had ceased by 1889. In 1901 the Llanwonno Colliery was reopened by Mr S.L. Jones, when the lower junction to the colliery siding was put in. On 12th March, 1901 the Traffic Committee approved an application from the Llanwonno Colliery Co., which had taken over Mr Jones' interest, for an upper junction to the siding. The colliery was linked to this siding by means of a short tramway, but proved extremely short-lived, as in October 1904 the TVR agreed to purchase the permanent way materials from the upper junction of the siding, the colliery having ceased working.

At the end of the branch the line divided into two short sidings, each ending in a mound of earth and being protected by chock blocks. TVR records give a 'Batchelor & Snowden's Siding', but nothing more is known of this particular user. In GWR days one of the sidings at the terminus was listed as a mileage siding, under the name of 'Llanwonno Siding', and saw very limited amounts of agricultural traffic, until closure in 1931.

Above Ynysybwl the branch had about it the air of a speculative line that had failed to develop the traffic for which it was intended. Although there were a number of small mines on this section over the years, these were very limited in scale and life span and can hardly have contributed to any significant extent towards the cost of pushing the railway into such an isolated and difficult area. In spite of these minor incursions, the railway and associated development hardly affected the peaceful rural character of the upper reaches of the valley.

The line between Stormstown Junction and Ynysybwl station had, at the opening to passengers in 1890, been worked by train staff and block telegraph. By the Grouping, however, it was worked on the electric train staff system, with the following sections:

Clydach Court Junction to Windsor Passing Siding:	Green Staff
Stormstown Junction to Windsor Passing Siding:	Red Staff
Windsor Passing Siding to Ynysybwl station:	Blue Staff

Between Ynysybwl and the end of the branch the line was worked by train staff with one engine in steam.

Chapter Eight

Decline and Fall

The first significant change in the organisation of the former TVR lines under the new regime came on 8th May, 1922, with the formation of the Cardiff Valleys Division of the GWR. The old TVR management were well represented in the new structure, with E. H. Dannatt, formerly Superintendent of the Line, appointed Divisional Superintendent. At the other end of the scale, evidence of the change in ownership came on 2nd October, 1922, when the title of 'Platform' gave way to the more usual 'Halt' on the Nelson and Ynysybwl branches and at other locations on the former TVR.

Passenger traffic on the two branches returned to reasonable levels after the restrictions of the war years. In 1923 a total of 56,899 tickets were sold at Ynysybwl and the four halts on that branch, together with 738 season tickets, whilst the comparable figures for the Nelson branch were 60,638 and 162. Most of the passenger business on the latter branch was concentrated at the Nelson end, the intermediate station of Cilfynydd contributing little as a result of the impact of intense tramway competition between that settlement and Pontypridd.

Originating freight traffic was also quite heavy, being predominantly coal from the three major collieries of Lady Windsor, Dowlais-Cardiff and Albion. In 1923 a total of 360,212 tons was handled on the Ynysybwl branch and 489,649 tons on the Nelson line. In addition, through traffic on the latter branch was well represented by the flow of iron ore from Llanharry Iron Ore Mine, on the Cowbridge branch, to Dowlais, which accounted for up to three loaded trains each day. In TVR days such traffic had been worked via Quaker's Yard, but with unified ownership, advantage could be taken of the most direct route between Pontypridd and Dowlais. The loss of this traffic in 1930, following the end of steel making at Dowlais, deprived the upper part of the Nelson branch of its major source of revenue and was undoubtedly an influential factor behind its subsequent closure. Potentially equally devastating, as far as the lower section of the branch was concerned, was the liquidation of the Albion Colliery Co. in 1928. Fortunately, this did not result in the end of coal mining at Cilfynydd, as ownership of the colliery passed to the Powell Duffryn Steam Coal Co. In 1935 this concern became part of Powell Duffryn Associated Collieries Ltd.

A further change in station nomenclature occurred on 1st July, 1924, when the GWR added '(Abercynon Upper)' to Travellers' Rest, presumably in an attempt to widen its potential catchment area, and '(Glam)' to Nelson, probably to avoid confusion with the English town of the same name.

Passenger traffic declined dramatically in the 1920s with the development of competing bus services and the increase in unemployment resulting from the onset of the Depression. The railway had always come a very poor second to the tramway between Pontypridd and Cilfynydd, and now the new bus services began to undermine the railway's competitive position over the longer

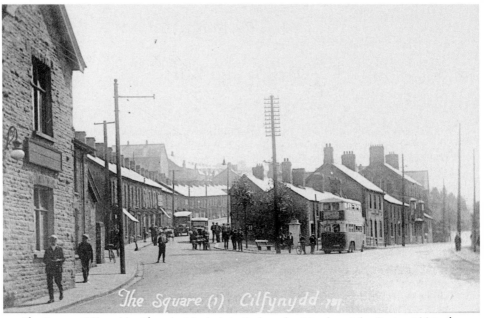

The Square, Cilfynydd with a double-deck trolleybus about to depart for Pontypridd in the 1930s. *Pontypridd Library*

The competition at Cilfynydd in the 1930s, with a single-deck trolleybus on the right. *Pontypridd Library*

distances to Nelson and Ynysybwl. The tramway itself was not immune to such changes, however, and in 1930 it was replaced by trolley buses between Pontypridd and Cilfynydd. By 1930 ticket sales on the Ynysybwl branch had fallen to only 14,718 per annum, or 26 per cent of the 1923 level, with season tickets down to 289. On the Nelson branch a similar picture was apparent, with ticket sales down to 30 per cent of the total for 1923, at 17,964 in 1930, with season tickets a derisory 23. The difference in the number of season tickets sold is accounted for by the fact that, by 1930, the Nelson trains had ceased to convey children on schools contracts.

Despite the drastic decline in the numbers of passengers using the trains on the branches, there had not been a corresponding reduction in staffing at Nelson, Cilfynydd and Ynysybwl stations. Ynysybwl had a staff of 12 in 1923, reducing to 10 in 1929 and eight by 1933; on the Nelson branch staff numbers fell from 11 in 1923 to seven in 1932.

One interesting feature of the traffic handled on the Ynysybwl branch in the 1920s was the significant number of livestock wagons dealt with for a coalfield valley branch line. Consistently over the decade the branch handled about 140 such wagons each year. However, this traffic faded away after 1931.

With the general decline in coal traffic after the Grouping the days of progressive expansion of facilities, which had been a constant feature since the opening of the TVR, gave way to a new period of retrenchment and rationalisation. As far as the Nelson and Ynysybwl branches were concerned, the swansong of the old days of major capital expenditure came in 1925 when extensive alterations were carried out at Stormstown Junction to enable shunting operations to be performed clear of the running lines. The sidings at Stormstown Junction were already quite substantial, with a capacity of 1,037 wagons recorded at the Grouping. More typical of the kind of changes which were to come, was the simplification carried out at the Merthyr end of Pontypridd station in 1928, when, on 28th October, the connection from the Rhondda branch to one of the short motor bays was taken out and the bay line diverted to join that from the Ynysybwl bay. In addition, by 1926, the complex layout at Ynysybwl station, with its short section of double line working, had also been simplified.

A more positive form of rationalisation appeared to be in prospect when, in June 1930, it was reported that alterations were to be carried out at Llancaiach Junction to enable trains from Pontypridd to Nelson to run through to Nelson and Llancaiach station. Although, according to the *GWR Magazine* of January 1931, this work was undertaken, the branch trains continued to terminate at Nelson station. After 1930 passenger traffic on the branch, already substantially reduced since the Grouping, declined still further, with a total of only 10,382 tickets being sold in 1931. With the end of steel making at Dowlais in 1930, the iron ore trains were taken off, leaving the meagre passenger service as the only traffic north of Cilfynydd. In these circumstances, the GWR appears to have taken the view that rather than attempt to rejuvenate the passenger service by extending trains through to Nelson and Llancaiach station, it would be wiser to cut its losses and withdraw the Pontypridd to Nelson service and close the section above Cilfynydd to all traffic. Accordingly, the passenger train service

Up Trains.   NELSON (Glam.) BRANCH.   Week Days only.

M.P. Mileage from Cardiff Docks	Distance from Pontypridd	STATIONS.	Station No.	Gradient. 1 in	Time allowances for Freight Trains. Stop.	Start.	Ordinary.	**B** Workmen's Auto Passenger. arr.	dep.	**B** Auto Passenger. arr.	dep.	**F** 8.0 a.m. Llantrisant to Ffaldcaiach Iron Ore. arr.	dep.
M. C.	M. C.							A.M.	A.M.	A.M.	A.M.	A.M.	A.M.
12 74	— —	Pontypridd	7610	277 R	—	—	—	—	5 43	—	6 57	—	—
13 56	0 62	Pont Shon Norton Junction	7960	L	—	2	—	C S		C S		8 50	8 58
13 75	1 1	Berw Road Halt	7646	430 F	—	—	—	5 45	5 46	6 59	7 0	—	—
14 67	1 73	Cilfynydd Loop Junction	7962	L	—	—	—	C S		C S		9 5B	E9 8
14 70	1 76	Albion Colliery Lower Junction		287 F	1	1	4	—	—	—	—		
15 13	2 19	Cilfynydd	7569	103 R	—	—	—	5 50	5 51	7 4	7 7		
— —	— —	Stormstown Junction	7972	178 R	—	—	—	—	—	—	—		
16 19	3 25	Ynysydwr Junction		40 R	—	—	—	—	—	—	—		
16 36	3 42	Traveller's Rest (Abercynon Upper)	7673	40 R	—	—	—	5-55	5 57	7 11	7 12		
18 11	5 17	Llanfabon Road Platform	7658	264 R	—	—	—	6 1	6 2	7 16	7 17		
18 41	5 47	Berthgron Siding	7963	550 R	—	—	—	—	—	—	—		
18 65	5 71	Nelson (Glam.)	7599	857 R	—	—	—	6 4	—	7 19	—	C 9¼S	
19 1	6 7	Nelson Goods	7965	215 R	1	—	15	—	—	—	—	9 24	
19 12	6 18	Llancaiach Junction		215 R	—	—	—	—	—	—	—	Z5	

STATIONS.	**F** 1.0 p.m. Llantrisant to Ffaldcaiach Iron Ore. arr.	dep.	**B** Passenger. arr.	dep.	**B** Passenger. arr.	dep.	**B** Passenger. SO arr.	dep.	**B** Passenger. SO arr.	dep.
			P.M.	P.M.	P.M.	P.M.	P.M.	P.M.	P.M.	P.M.
Pontypridd			—	3 17	—	5 21	—	8 33	—	10 55
Pont Shon Norton Junction	C 1s6S		C S		C S		C S		C S	
Berw Road Halt			3 19	3 20	5 23	5 24	8 35	8 36	10 57	10 58
Cilfynydd Loop Junction	1 55	2 37	C S		C S		C S		C S	
Albion Colliery Lower Junction										
Cilfynydd			3 24	2 ??	5 28	5 29	8 40	8 41	11 2	11 3
Stormstown Junction										
Ynysydwr Junction										
Traveller's Rest (Abercynon Upper)			3 29	3 30	5 33	5 34	8 45	8 46	11 7	11 8
Llanfabon Road Platform			3 34	3 35	5 38	5 39	8 50	8 51	11 12	11 13
Berthgron Siding										
Nelson (Glam.)	C 2⅛S		3 37	—	5 41	—	8 55	—	11 15	—
Nelson Goods										
Llancaiach Junction	3 55									

Down Trains.   NELSON (GLAM.) BRANCH.   Week Days only.
Single Line Pont Shon Norton Junction and Nelson (Glam.), worked by Electric Train Staff.   Staff Stations—Pont Shon Norton Junction, Cilfynydd Loop. Nelson.   Crossing Station—Cilfynydd Loop.

Distance from Llancaiach Junction.	STATIONS.	Station No.	Gradient. 1 in	Time Allowances for Freight Trains. Stop.	Start.	Ordinary.	**B** Workmen's Auto Passenger. arr.	dep.	**B** Auto Passenger. arr.	dep.	**F** 10.10 a.m. Ffaldcaiach to Llantrisant Empties. arr.	dep.
M. C.							A.M.	A.M.	A.M.	A.M.	A.M.	A.M.
— —	Llancaiach Junction	7965	215 F.	—	—	—	—	—	—	—	10 14	
0 11	Nelson Goods	7965	215 F.	—	1	—	—	—	—	—		
-0 27	Nelson (Glam.)	7599	857 F.	—	—	—	—	6 15	—	—	C 10 18S	
1 1	Llanfabon Road Platform	7658	26- F.	—	—	—	6 17	6 19	7 36	7 37	P	
	Stop Board			—	—	—	—	—	—	—	P	
2 56	Traveller's Rest (Abercynon Upper)	7673	40 F.	—	—	—	6 23	6 25	7 41	7 42	SUS-PENDED	
2 73	Ynysydwr Junction		40 F.	—	—	—	—	—	—	—		
— —	Stormstown Junction	7972	178 F.	—	—	—	—	—	—	—		
3 79	Cilfynydd	7569	103 F.	—	—	—	6 29	6 31	7 46	7 47		
4 25	Cilfynydd Loop Junction	7962	-L	1	1	24	C S		C S		1044P	10 47
5 17	Berw Road Halt	7646	430 F.	—	—	—	6 35	6 36	7 51	7 52		
6 36	Pont Shon Norton Junction	7960	25 R.	1	—	8	C S		C S		C 10 58S	
6 18	Pontypridd	7910	277 F.	—	—	—	6 38	—	7 55	—	Z 5	

STATIONS.	**B** Passenger. SO arr.	dep.	**F** Llantwit-Passenger. SX arr.	dep.	3.30 p.m. Ffaldcaiach to Llantrisant Empties. arr.	dep.	**B** Passenger. arr.	dep.	**B** Passenger. SO arr.	dep.	**B** Passenger. SO arr.	dep.
	P.M.	P.M.	P.M.	P.M.	P.M.	P.M.	P.M.	P.M.	P.M.	P.M.	P.M.	P.M.
Llancaiach Junction						3 35						
Nelson Goods												
Nelson (Glam.)	—	3 50	—	4 10	3 38*	4 30	—	5 49	—	9 5	—	11 25
Llanfabon Road Platform	3 52	3 55	4 12	4 13	—	—	5 51	5 52	9 7	9 8		
Stop Board					P	—						
Traveller's Rest (Abercynon Upper)	3 57	3 58	4 17	4 18	SUS-PENDED		5 56	5 57	9 12	9 13		
Ynysydwr Junction												
Stormstown Junction												
Cilfynydd	4 2	4 3	4 22	4 23	—	—	6 1	6 2	9 17	9 18		
Cilfynydd Loop Junction	C S		C S		4 56P	4 59	C S		C S		C S	
Berw Road Halt	4 7	4 8	4 27	4 28	—	—	6 6	6 7	9 22	9 23		
Pont Shon Norton Junction	C S		C S		C 5 1S		C S		C S		C S	
Pontypridd	4 10	—	4 30	4 32	—	—	6 9	—	9 25	—	11 37	

GWR Working Timetable, September 1930.   *Courtesy R. Darleston*

Down Trains.   YNYSYBWL BRANCH.   Week Days Only.

Distance.	STATIONS.	Station No.	Gradient 1 in	Time Allowance for Freight Trains.			B — Cardiff (Clar. Rd.) Auto Passenger.		B — Auto Passenger.		K — 9.40 a.m. Mynachdy Goods.		B — Auto Passenger.		B — Auto Passenger.		B — Auto Passenger.		B — Auto Passenger.	
				Stop.	Start.	Ordinary.	arr.	dep.	arr.	dep.	arr.	dep.	arr.	dep.	arr.	dep.	arr.	dep.	arr.	dep.
M. C.							A.M.	A.M.	A.M.	A.M.	A.M.	A.M.	A.M.	A.M.			A.M.	A.M.	P.M.	P.M.
	Old Ynysybwl Halt	7663	59 F	—	1	—	—	7 35	—	9 5	—	P	—	10 35	—	—	—	11 52	—	1 0	—	1 55
	Stop Board																			
38	Ynysybwl Quarry Siding	7970	51 F	2	1	1														
48	Ynysybwl	7638	51 F	2	1	—	7 37	7 38	9 7	9 8	9 45	9 50	10 37	10 38	11 54	11 55	1 2	1 3	1 57	1 58
73	Robertstown Halt	7667	66 F	—	—	—	7 40	7 41	9 10	9 11	—	—	10 40	10 41	11 57	11 58	1 5	1 6	2 0	2 1
1 28	Ynysybwl (New Road) Halt	7676	66 F	—	—	—	7 43	7 44	9 13	9 14	—	—	10 43	10 44	12 0	12 1	1 8	1 9	2 3	2 4
1 32	Windsor Siding	7965	66 F	2	5	3	CS		CS		P		CS		CS		CS		CS	
	Stop Board		66 F																	
2 37	Clydach Court Halt	7649	47 F	—	—	—	7 46	7 47	—	9 17										
2 54	Clydach Court Junction	7966	412 F	1	2	9	CS		CS		—		CS		CS		CS		CS	
4 41	Pontypridd	7610	277 F	—	—	—	7 52	7 55	9 22	—	10 4	—	10 50	—	12 7	—	1 15	—	2 10	—
	Stormstown	7972	348 F				....	....	....	....	10 4	—								
	Abercynon	7552	692 R				....	....	....	....	J 6									

STATIONS.	B — Auto Passenger.			B — Auto Passenger.		B — Auto Passenger.		B — Auto Passenger.		B — Auto Passenger. SO		B — Auto Passenger.		B — Auto Passenger. SO		B — Auto Passenger.	
	arr.	dep.		arr.	dep.	arr.	dep.	arr.	dep.	arr.	dep.	arr.	dep.	arr.	dep.	arr.	dep.
	P.M.	P.M.		P.M.	P.M.	P.M.	P.M.	P.M.	P.M.	P.M.	P.M.	P.M.	P.M.	P.M.	P.M.	P.M.	P.M.
Old Ynysybwl Halt	—	2 0		—	5 8	—	5 50	—	7 31	—	—	—	9 0	—	—	—	11 10
Stop Board																	
Ynysybwl Quarry Siding																	
Ynysybwl	4 2	4 3		5 10	5 11	5 52	5 53	7 33	7 34	8 17	—	9 2	9 3	9 53	9 55	11 12	11 13
Robertstown Halt	4 5	4 6		5 13	5 14	5 55	5 56	7 36	7 37	—	—	9 4	9 6	9 55	9 56	11 15	11 16
Ynysybwl (New Road) Halt	4 8	4 9		5 16	5 17	5 58	5 59	7 39	7 40	—	—	9 8	9 9	9 58	9 59	11 18	11 19
Windsor Siding	CS			CS		CS		CS		—		CS		CS		CS	
Stop Board																	
Clydach Court Halt								7 42	7 43	—		9 11	9 12				
Clydach Court Junction	CS			CS		CS		CS		—		CS		CS		CS	
Pontypridd	4 15	—		5 23	—	6 5	—	7 52	—	8 37	—	9 17	—	10 5	—	11 25	—
Stormstown	....																
Abercynon	....																

Up Trains.   YNYSYBWL BRANCH.   Week Days Only.
Single Line—

Clydach Court Junction and Windsor Siding. \ Electric   Ynysybwl and Old Ynysybwl.   Train Staff.   One engine in steam.
Stormstown Junction and Windsor Siding. > Train   Old Ynysybwl and end of)   Mineral Line only.
Windsor Siding and Ynysybwl. / Staff.   Branch.

Mile Post from Cardiff Docks	Mileage from Pontypridd Pass. Station	STATIONS.	Station No.	Gradient 1 in	Time Allowance for Freight Trains.			B — Auto Passenger.		K — Goods. J6		B — Auto Passenger.		B — Auto Passenger.		B — Auto Passenger.	
					Stop.	Start.	Ordinary.	arr.	dep.	arr.	dep.	arr.	dep.	arr.	dep.	arr.	dep.
M. C.	M. C.							A.M.	A.M.	A.M.	A.M.	A.M.	A.M.	A.M.	A.M.	P.M.	P.M.
16 28	3 34	Abercynon	7552	692 F				....	....	8 0	—						
12 74		Stormstown	7972	348 F						—	—						
12 74		Pontypridd	7610	277 R				—	7 15	—	—	8 42	—	10 15	—	11 32	—	12 35
14 61	1 67	Clydach Court Junction	7966	412 R	—	1	—	CS		—	—	CS		CS		CS	
14 78	2 4	Clydach Court Halt	7649	66 R	—	1	10	—	—	8 47	8 48	—	—	—	—	12 40	12 41
15 73	2 79	Darraddu		66 R				—	—	8 12							
16 3	3 9	Windsor Siding	7965	66 R	—	—	—	CS		8 40	—	CS		CS		CS	
16 7	3 43	Ynysybwl (New Road) Halt	7676	66 R	1	—	1	7 22	7 23	—	8 52	8 53	10 22	10 23	11 39	11 40	12 45	12 46
16 42	3 48	Robertstown Halt	7667	66 R	—	—	—	7 26	7 27	—	8 55	8 57	10 26	10 27	11 43	11 44	12 49	12 50
16 67	3 73	Ynysybwl	7638	51 R	1	—	4	7 30	7 31	8 46	9 20	9 0	10 30	10 31	11 47	11 48	12 53	12 54
16 77	4 2	Ynysybwl Quarry Siding	7970	51 R	—	—	—	—	—	9 22	9 30						
17 36	4 41	Old Ynysybwl Halt	7663	59 R	1	1	2	7 33	—	9 32	—	9 3	—	10 33	—	11 50	—	12 56
17 66	4 72	Mynachdy		40 R	1		1										

STATIONS.	B — Auto Passenger.		B — Auto Passenger.		B — Auto Passenger.		B — Auto Passenger.		B — Auto Passenger. SX		B — Auto Passenger. SO		B — Auto Passenger. SO		B — Auto Passenger.		B — Auto Passenger. SO	
	arr.	dep.	arr.	dep.	arr.	dep.	arr.	dep.	arr.	dep.	arr.	dep.	arr.	dep.	arr.	dep.	arr.	dep.
	P.M.	P.M.	P.M.	P.M.	P.M.	P.M.	P.M.	P.M.	P.M.	P.M.	P.M.	P.M.	P.M.	P.M.	P.M.	P.M.	P.M.	P.M.
Abercynon	....		....															
Stormstown	....		....															
Pontypridd	—	1 35	—	2 33	—	6 45	—	5 28	—	6 45	—	8 55	—	8 0	—	8 37	—	9 31	—	10 48
Clydach Court Junction	CS		CS		CS		CS		CS		CS		CS		CS		CS	
Clydach Court Halt	—	—	—	—	4 50	4 51	—	—	6 50	6 51	7 0	7 1	—	—	8 42	8 43	—	—	—	—
Darraddu																		
Windsor Siding	CS		CS		CS		CS		CS		CS		CS		CS		CS	
Ynysybwl (New Road) Halt	1 42	1 43	3 45	3 46	4 55	4 56	5 35	5 36	6 55	6 56	7 5	7 6	8 47	8 48	9 58	9 59	10 55	10 56
Robertstown Halt	1 46	1 47	3 49	3 50	4 59	5 0	5 39	5 40	6 59	7 0	7 9	7 10	8 51	8 52	9 42	9 43	10 59	11 0
Ynysybwl	1 50	1 51	3 53	3 54	5 3	5 4	5 43	5 44	7 3	7 4	7 13	7 14	8 15	—	8 55	8 56	9 46	—	11 3	11 4
Ynysybwl Quarry Siding																		
Old Ynysybwl Halt	1 53	—	3 56	—	5 6	—	5 46	—	7 6	—	7 16	—	—	—	8 58	—	....		11 6	—
Mynachdy																		

GWR Working Timetable, September 1930.   *Courtesy R. Darleston*

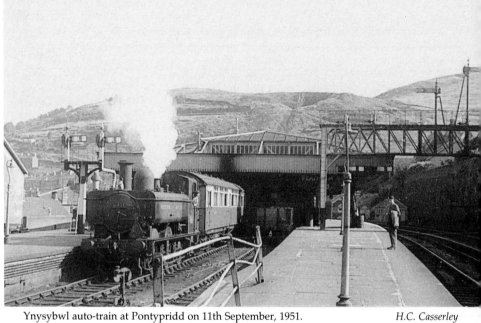

Ynysybwl auto-train at Pontypridd on 11th September, 1951.   *H.C. Casserley*

The Ynysybwl auto-train at Pontypridd Junction on 26th July, 1952.   *R.C. Riley*

The scene of destruction at Old Ynysybwl Halt on 11th September, 1951.   *H.C. Casserley*

SLS Special formed of ex-GWR 0-6-0PT No. 6423 and two ex-TVR auto-trailers at the remains of Cilfynydd station on 12th July, 1952.   *H.T. Hobbs*

The site of Travellers' Rest station on the Nelson branch. *Real Photographs*

Nature regains its own at Nelson station. By this time the track had been cut back to the bridge in the background. *L&GRP*

was withdrawn on 12th September, 1932.

There being no Sunday service, the last trains ran on Saturday, 10th September, when the line saw the customary last day crowds eager to bid their farewells. So much so that it was said at the time that the takings were a record for any single day since the opening to passengers in 1900. The passenger service between Pontypridd and Nelson had lasted a mere 32 years.

Following the withdrawal of the passenger train service, the line between Albion Colliery, Cilfynydd, and Nelson was closed to all traffic, together with the connections from this section to Dowlais-Cardiff Colliery and Stormstown Junction. At the Nelson end a short section of the branch, together with the former run-round loop, were retained as sidings from Llancaiach Junction.

Initially, the line from Llancaiach Junction was left in place to a point just beyond the Pontypridd end of Nelson station platform, but was later cut back to about the bridge carrying Commercial Street over the railway. For a time the station building was used as a railwaymen's institute. During World War II it was used by the Home Guard and ended its days as a storeroom for a local ironmonger, before being demolished. At Stormstown Junction the connection from the ex-TVR main line was retained to provide access to the Dowlais-Cardiff Colliery and adjoining sidings on the branch, near the junction. The rest of the line was dismantled between late 1935 and 1938, with the exception of the section from Dowlais-Cardiff Junction to the upper junction to the Albion Colliery, at Cilfynydd, which was sold to Powell Duffryn Associated Collieries Ltd on 11th January, 1936, before being reduced to the status of a siding on 3rd October, 1938. The date of its final closure is not known, but the disused length of track from a point just beyond the upper junction to Albion Colliery to near the site of the Dowlais-Cardiff Junction was still in place in 1968, complete with TVR permanent way materials.

The passenger train service on the Ynysybwl branch survived the minor massacre of unremunerative branch lines in South Wales in the early 1930s: indeed the traffic increased slightly during these years, with a total of 20,000 tickets being sold in 1933. The Winter timetable of 14th September, 1931 saw the introduction of a morning train from Old Ynysybwl Halt to Abercynon for the benefit of school children. In the opposite direction a Pontypridd-Old Ynysybwl train was diverted via Abercynon in the late afternoon. These trains restored, albeit in a very limited form, the direct link between Ynysybwl and Abercynon which had come to an end with the introduction of the motor car service in 1904.

The upper part of the Ynysybwl branch, above Mynachdy Colliery, had always been very poorly used. Apart from some coal from the short-lived and small-scale collieries at Black Grove and Llanwonno, little traffic had ever been generated by this forlorn relic of the speculative policies of earlier years. After the demise of the collieries all that was left was a tiny quantity of agricultural traffic handled at Cwm Clydach and Llanwonno mileage sidings. This came to an end in 1931 and the line above Mynachdy Colliery was removed in December 1938. Following the termination of the private siding agreement to Mynachdy Colliery in 1942, the section above Old Ynysybwl Halt was closed completely on 22nd September, 1949, with the track being taken up in March 1950.

Clydach Court Junction on 25th May, 1959, after the removal of the connections to the Clydach Court Loop.   *M. Hale*

Seven years after the passage of the last passenger train, Clydach Court Halt remains surprisingly intact on 25th August, 1959.   *M. Hale*

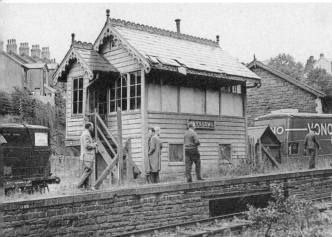

Above: A diesel railcar set on an SLS special at the upper junction to Albion Colliery sidings on 11th July, 1958. The track in the foreground had originally run through to Nelson.   *I.L. Wright*

Left: Ynysybwl signal box, retained as a ground frame, 11th July, 1959.   *J.J. Davis*

Below: The end of the line at Ynysybwl on 11th July, 1959.   *D.K. Jones Collection*

The camera attracts more attention than the novelty of a dmu on an excursion working at Ynysybwl on 11th July, 1959. *I.L. Wright*

The remains of Cilfynydd station alongside Albion Colliery, 29th July, 1960. *M. Hale*

The introduction of petrol rationing during World War II brought with it a return of passenger traffic to the railway, but this proved short-lived, and with the coming of peace and the restoration of the high-frequency bus service between Ynysybwl and Pontypridd, passengers quickly deserted the branch line. There was one final flourish, in retrospect a clear sign of impending closure, when in 1949, not long after Nationalisation, the old platform at Old Ynysybwl Halt was swept away and replaced by a new structure, capable of holding a two-car auto-set. Unfortunately, in the process, the old waiting shed was removed, leaving intending passengers without any form of shelter. To complete this scene of change and destruction, the overbridge just beyond the halt was taken down and replaced by a rough earth bank between the stone abutments.

Somewhat surprisingly, the Ynysybwl branch passenger train service, by then more or less moribund, survived the spate of temporary closures which occurred during the fuel crisis in the early part of 1951. However, the timetable was not restored to pre-war levels; on the contrary, it was progressively reduced after 1950, and from 30th June, 1952 comprised only five trains each way, with three extra return trips on Saturdays only. A total of three trains were routed via Abercynon. Unfortunately, the spacing of trains in the weekday timetable was such that the service was only of use to those attending school or working in Pontypridd; it was of very little use to shoppers unless they were prepared to spend a minimum of seven hours in Pontypridd. Nevertheless, the proposal to withdraw the passenger train service, which was made towards the end of 1951, provoked considerable local protest. However, the figures produced to justify closure told a rather different story: it was clear that very little use was being made of the trains. On one particular day passenger takings at Ynysybwl had amounted to only 1s. 3d., with those for the entire month coming to about £40. Withdrawal of the service was fixed for Monday, 28th July, 1952. In the absence of a Sunday service, Saturday, 26th July saw the usual last day crowds, with that odd mixture of perverse celebration and sad reflection. It being a Saturday, the full timetable was in operation and the last train left Pontypridd at 9.42 pm to the cry of 'Any more for the last Bwl train?' Large crowds witnessed its passing at Robertstown and Ynysybwl and at Old Ynysybwl Halt, from where the last timetabled train departed for Pontypridd at 10.03 pm.

The withdrawal of the passenger service resulted in the complete closure of the four halts on the branch, but Ynysybwl station remained open for goods traffic. Latterly, the station signal box was downgraded to the status of a ground frame, although the signals remained in place. The section of line from Ynysybwl to Old Ynysybwl Halt was closed to all traffic after the last passenger train in 1952, but it was not taken up until July 1957. Also closed to all traffic following the ending of the passenger service was Clydach Court Loop, but here again there was no rush to lift the track, which was left in place, becoming increasingly overgrown, until it was removed in 1959. Clydach Court Junction signal box remained in use after closure of the loop line, eventually closing on 6th November, 1962.

Excursions continued to be run from Ynysybwl for some years after cessation

The north end of Abercynon station on 13th April, 1963, with the main line to Merthyr climbing away on the right of the picture and the Aberdare branch curving away to the left. The siding off the Aberdare line in the centre of the picture was used to stable Ynysybwl branch trains.

M. Hale

Double-headed English Electric class '37s' Nos. 37 280 and 37 275 are seen loading wagons at Lady Windsor Colliery prior to heading a 'Merry-go-round' train to Aberthaw, July 1986.

Dr. M. Rhodes

A Cardiff-Merthyr dmu service passes Stormstown Junction on 30th June, 1982. In the distance an English Electric class '37' runs round its Lady Windsor Colliery-Radyr train made up of unfitted coal wagons.

Dr M. Rhodes

A view looking along the branch towards Lady Windsor Colliery with the bridge over the River Clydach in the foreground in 1988. *Paul Joyce*

The Monmouthshire Railway Society railtour is seen heading towards Lady Windsor Colliery on 15th October, 1988. *Paul Joyce*

of the regular passenger service in 1952. One such train was a return special from Barry Island on 2nd June, 1956, hauled by class '56XX' 0-6-2T No. 5601.

Ynysybwl goods yard, latterly used as a rail distribution depot by Vono Bedding of Tipton, in the West Midlands, was closed on 2nd November, 1959, together with the line from the station to Windsor Passing Siding. This section was finally taken out of use on 12th June, 1960, when Windsor Passing Siding signal box was closed. Henceforth, the branch line's role was confined to that of a mineral railway linking Lady Windsor Colliery to the main line at Stormstown Junction. Lady Windsor was regarded as a long-life pit and saw substantial investment over the years. In 1974 it was connected by underground link to the Dowlais-Cardiff Colliery at Abercynon. This brought more traffic to the Ynysybwl branch, but at the expense of the siding to Dowlais-Cardiff Colliery, which was taken out of use. The closure of the Clydach Court Loop meant that all traffic from the remaining part of the Ynysybwl branch had to be dealt with at Stormstown Junction. This enabled all shunting movements for Lady Windsor and Dowlais-Cardiff Collieries' traffic to be concentrated at one place, but the reversal it entailed later became something of a handicap with the introduction of block coal trains on 'merry-go-round' workings from Lady Windsor Colliery to Aberthaw power stations. Stormstown Junction signal box was closed on 12th August, 1977, when control of the junction itself was transferred to Abercynon signal box.

On the Pont Shon Norton branch, Albion Colliery closed on 2nd September, 1966, but the railway remained in use for the removal of coal stocks. The branch was taken out of use in October 1969, but re-opened on 24th November of that year to enable further coal stocks to be brought out. The branch finally closed on 14th September, 1970, Pont Shon Norton Junction signal box having been replaced by a ground frame in the preceding June.

The ending of the national coal strike in 1985 saw the start of the final rundown of the deep mined coal industry of South Wales. Lady Windsor Colliery closed on 26th March, 1988, production having come to an end five weeks earlier. Rail traffic continued for a while longer, however, taking out coal which had been stockpiled at the pit. The last such working from the colliery took place on 20th May, 1988, but a final revenue-earning train passed over the line on 15th October of that year. This took the form of an enthusiasts' excursion, organised by the Monmouthshire Railway Society, to commemorate the passing of this last section of the Ynysybwl branch line. The branch was clipped out of use on 9th October, 1990.

Class 'M' 0-6-2T No. 162, built Kitson & Co., 1886. *WRRC Collection*

TVR class 'N' 0-6-2T No. 188, built Kitson & Co., 1891. *Welsh Industrial and Maritime Museum*

Chapter Nine

Locomotive and Train Working

The original Llancaiach branch was laid out so as to be suitable for horse-drawn traffic. Its rope-worked inclined plane, near the junction with the TVR main line, compensated for the dramatic change of levels between the valley floor and the hillside route to Llancaiach and enabled horses to perform with reasonable efficiency over the relatively level railway above the incline. Horse power did not last for long, however, as can be seen from the TVR Superintendent's report of 30th May, 1844, in which he states that, 'I find that the present stock of engines consists of eight, one is constantly required above the plane (i.e. Main Incline) and another on the Llancaiach Branch'. A further report, dated 17th June, 1844, refers to the continuance of the use of one of Hawthorn's 'patent engines' on the branch. The engines in question were four 0-4-2 mineral engines, *Dinas*, *Dowlais*, *Llancaiach* and *Plymouth*, supplied by R. & W. Hawthorn in 1841. The same report noted that not every engine could work over the branch because of the presence of a very sharp curve, near St Cynon's Church, and a very low bridge. On 15th January, 1845 instructions were given to raise the height of the bridge concerned, but it is not clear whether this was, in fact, done, as the TVR working instructions for 1856 refer to the engine used on the Llancaiach branch being fitted with a hinged chimney, which could be lowered to pass under a low bridge.

On 10th December, 1845 the TVR decided to purchase an engine belonging to colliery owner Thomas Powell. Powell had acquired this engine about May 1842 with the intention of employing it to work his traffic over the TVR, something which the TVR was not prepared to countenance. Following this rebuff, Powell made use of this engine on his Lantwit Vardre Railway, to the south of Pontypridd, for a while, before reverting to horse power on that line. In June 1844 he offered the TVR the use of the engine, named *Llantwit*, in exchange for the loan of wagons for his traffic, an arrangement which was followed, in December 1845, by its outright purchase for the sum of £580. *Llantwit* was built by Messrs C. & J. Rennie, with 12 in. x 18 in. cylinders, suggesting an engine of 1838 vintage. TVR records describe it as a 6-wheel, 4-coupled locomotive, with 4 ft 6 in. driving wheels. It is not known if *Llantwit* was used on the Llancaiach branch from the date at which it passed to the TVR, but what is certain, from TVR records, is that it was used as the principal engine on the branch between 1850 and 1856. *Llantwit* was withdrawn in 1858.

Two other engines, usually substituting for *Llantwit*, were recorded on the Llancaiach branch during this period. *Dinas*, one of the Hawthorn 0-4-2s already referred to, was there in 1856, whilst *Gloucester*, an American-built 4-2-0 purchased second-hand from the Birmingham & Gloucester Railway in 1845, is listed as a spare engine for the branch from 1853 to 1856.

Judging from the plans deposited for the TVR Act of 1873, there appears to have been a small engine shed on the Llancaiach branch, just above the top of the incline. In January 1853 the construction of an engine shed at Aberdare

TVR class 'O1' 0-6-2T No. 78, built Kitson & Co., 1894. *LCGB*

Class 'O4' No. 1, built Vulcan Foundry, 1910, at Abercynon, *c.* 1920. *LCGB*

Junction was approved, in connection with shunting requirements at the foot of the Main Incline. This shed was to survive through to 1928, by which time its very limited facilities had become totally inadequate in relation to the size of its locomotive allocation.

No details have come to light concerning the types of locomotives used on the original Llancaiach branch after 1856. However, given the self-contained nature of working on the branch, together with the short distance involved, it is reasonable to assume that older, smaller engines were the typical motive power. One of the operating advantages of the diversion of Llancaiach coal traffic via Quaker's Yard in 1870 was that larger engines could be used over longer distances.

Before leaving the original Llancaiach branch reference should be made to the inclined plane itself, strictly speaking an aspect of motive power on the branch. The double-tracked plane was worked on the balanced load principle, whereby loaded wagons running down the incline drew up empty wagons to which they were attached by a rope which passed over a wheel at the top of the incline. This wheel was housed below rail level and there are a number of instances recorded of it breaking or being out of repair, resulting in long periods of inactivity at the incline. It was not until March 1844 that the precaution of having a duplicate set cast was agreed, so that any stoppage could quickly be remedied. Apart from the problems which resulted from such interruptions, the balanced load principle placed severe constraints on the capacity of the inclined plane. It appears that the Llancaiach branch engine was restricted to the section above the incline; no evidence has been found to suggest that engines worked up the inclined plane, assisted by the rope, as was the case on the Main Incline after 1849 and, in later years, the Pwllyrhebog Incline, in the Rhondda Fawr Valley, which was also worked on the balanced load principle.

Following the diversion of the Llancaiach coal traffic via Quaker's Yard in 1870, there was a gap of about 15 years before Stormstown Junction (as it became) regained the status of an important traffic centre. Although the junction itself was re-instated in 1878, it was not until the opening of the Ynysybwl branch that traffic of any significance was handled at Stormstown. Traffic on the Ynysybwl branch would probably have been worked by 0-6-0 tank engines: Ahrons notes that most of the early tank engines of this type were found on the upper reaches and the branches of the TVR at this date. In 1885 the TVR introduced the first of a type which was to become characteristic of the company - the 0-6-2 tank engine (later classes 'M' and 'M1'). At first these engines worked heavier main line passenger trains, but with the increasing availability of this type, after 1890, such tank engines came to be seen on branch line passenger and goods trains, as well.

On 31st December, 1889 an additional engine and set of carriages, together with crew, were despatched from Cardiff Cathays Shed to Aberdare Junction for the introduction of the passenger train service on the Ynysybwl branch on the following day. The inaugural timetable comprised only three trains each way, with the engine running light from Aberdare Junction to Ynysybwl at the beginning of the day to collect the carriages which were stabled in the carriage siding at the branch terminus. This pattern of working continued until the

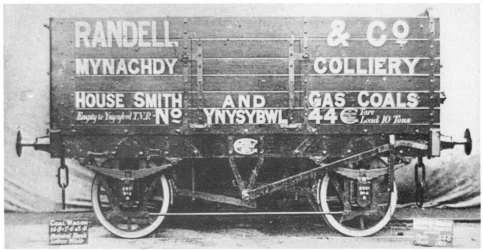

Above: A private owner wagon belonging to the owner of the original Mynachdy Colliery on the Ynysybwl branch. *HMRS*

Right: A typical 'Ocean' coal wagon which would have been seen in vast numbers at Lady Windsor Colliery on the Ynysybwl branch. *HMRS*

Below: The later Mynachdy Colliery gave great prominence to its name on its private owner wagons. *HMRS*

introduction of the motor car service in 1904. Prior to this, passenger trains were made up of 4-wheeled coaches dating from the 1870s and 1880s, with a brake van at each end. The working instructions in force on the branch required there to be a guard and a brakesman on each passenger train. The first such set of instructions recorded the names of the gentlemen involved: Palmer Richards and Reuben Owens. When not required on the passenger service, this pair were to carry out duties on the mineral trains on the branch. Mineral and goods traffic was to be brought down the line from the various sidings to Windsor Passing Siding, from where it was to be cleared by the Ynysybwl mineral engine, when taking out 'Ocean' coal for Stormstown Junction. The early 0-6-2T engines were, of course, ideally suited to a mixed traffic mode of working.

By July 1891 three additional return trips, running Wednesdays and Saturdays only, had been added to the Ynysybwl branch timetable. These were subsequently consolidated, by 1897, to give a total of six trains each way, Mondays to Saturdays. On the freight side, the working timetable for April 1897 shows that two pilot engines, one working during the day and the other covering night duties, were required to clear out traffic from the various sidings and bring traffic down to Stormstown Junction, from where it was to be picked up by main line trains. On the Llancaiach branch this timetable gives a solitary goods train each way, daily, between Stormstown Junction and Llancaiach, hauled by an Abercynon engine. Having dealt with the Llancaiach branch traffic, this train then picked up wagons from the Dowlais-Cardiff Colliery, before working through to Cardiff Docks. Traffic to and from Albion Colliery on the Pont Shon Norton branch was handled by engines from Cardiff Cathays shed.

When passenger trains were introduced on the Nelson branch in 1900 the mode of working differed from that of the Ynysybwl branch in that the carriages were not stabled at the branch terminus. Nelson branch passenger trains were also made up of elderly 4-wheeled stock, hauled by 0-6-2T engines, usually of classes 'M1' or 'O1'. On 16th July, 1900 the Traffic Committee approved the alteration, at an estimated cost of £56, of two 4-wheeled brake third class carriages, Nos. 227 and 228 (built by the Oldbury Railway Carriage Co. in 1885) for use on the branch instead of brake composites. Later that year, on 29th September, the committee accepted an application for the provision of a workmen's train between Nelson and Travellers' Rest (where a station was required) to serve the Dowlais-Cardiff Colliery. At first this service was advertised only between Nelson and Travellers' Rest, but was later shown as running through to Pontypridd. In June 1901 the Nelson branch service comprised six trains in each direction between Pontypridd and Nelson, together with a short working to and from Cilfynydd and the workmen's service already referred to.

Following the opening of the Clydach Court Loop in 1900 'Ocean' coal traffic from Lady Windsor Colliery was worked directly from the colliery to Treforest (Barry) Junction for exchange with the Barry Railway. The working timetable for 1903 includes four such workings, all handled by Abercynon engines. At this date no regular workings were shown on the Nelson branch, above Ynysydwr Junction. Cardiff engines still predominated on Albion Colliery trains and also worked a Dowlais-Cardiff Colliery to Cathays trip, via

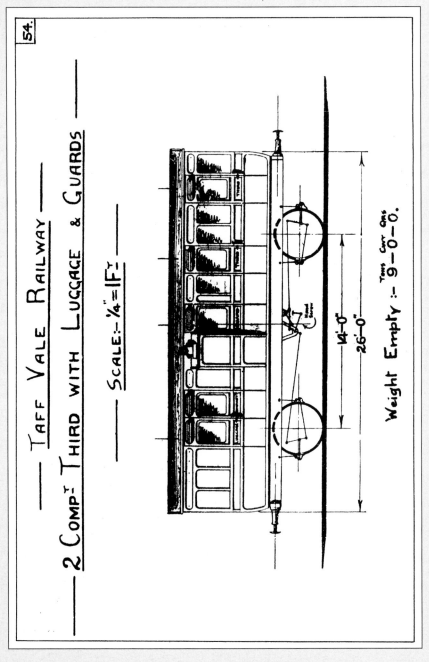

54.

TAFF VALE RAILWAY

2 Compᵗ Third with Luggage & Guards

Scale:- ¼"=1Fᵗ

14'-0"

26'-0"

Weight Empty :- 9-0-0. Tons Cwt Qrs

TVR diagram of third class brake coach No. 228. On 16th July, 1900 the TVR Traffic Committee agreed 'A recommendation for altering, at an estimated cost of £56, third class brake coaches Nos. 227 and 228 for use instead of brake composite coaches on the Llancaiach Branch'.

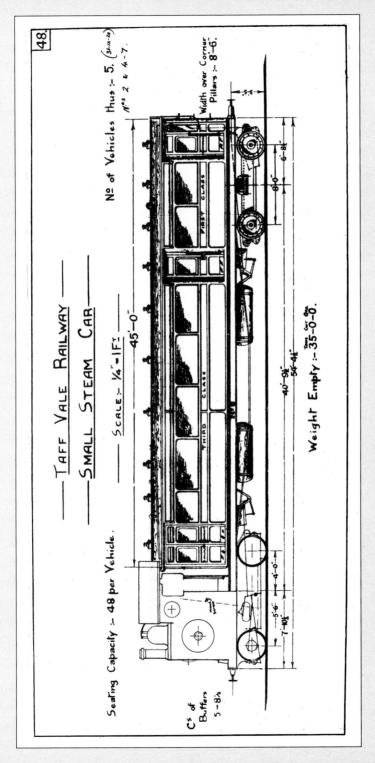

TVR diagram of steam motor car.

The rural surroundings at Old Ynysybwl provide the backdrop for TVR Motor Car No. 11 as its crew pose for the camera *c.* 1910. *R.C. Riley Collection*

Locomotive unit No. 6 coupled to large coach unit No. 16 at Old Ynysybwl *c.* 1910. *C.W. Harris Collection*

Cilfynydd. In addition, an Abercynon engine worked through from Dowlais-Cardiff Colliery, via Albion Colliery, to Roath Line Junction.

Prior to the introduction of Motor Car No. 1 on an experimental service on the Penarth branch on 21st December 1903, the car made a number of trial runs over various parts of the TVR system, including the Nelson branch. On 5th November, 1903 Car No. 1 conveyed Albion Colliery Co. Directors to Cilfynydd, where it ran into the colliery siding, before continuing up the branch to Nelson. Also on board were Mr Harland, the TVR Traffic Manager, Mr Cameron, Deputy Locomotive Superintendent and Mr Hallet, Deputy Traffic Superintendent. Another trial run worked to Nelson on 16th December, 1903, but no record has been found of such a trip on the Ynysybwl branch, although this is not to say that one did not take place.

The first 'production' cars (Nos. 2-7) were built by the Avonside Engine Co. of Bristol (engine units) and the Bristol Wagon & Carriage Co. (coach units) and catered for first and second class passengers. Their arrival from the builders from July 1904 enabled motor car services to be commenced on the Nelson and Ynysybwl branches. A number of other services had to wait until 1905, when the second batch of cars appeared. This build (Nos. 8-13) came from Kerr, Stuart & Co. (engine units) and the Bristol Wagon & Carriage Co. (coach units) and were intended for third class passengers only. The Nelson and Ynysybwl services were designated for third class only, but all types of cars appeared, with or without first class accommodation.

On the Nelson branch the cars shared the service with ordinary trains, in addition to the workmen's trains. There seems to have been a certain lack of confidence, on the part of the TVR, in the case of this particular service, as witnessed by the following notice which was attached to the passenger timetable: 'The Motor Car service is provisional and experimental, and the Company do not bind themselves to the continuance thereof.'

Ordinary trains also continued to appear on the Ynysybwl branch when traffic outstripped the accommodation provided by the motor cars, especially on Saturdays. However, such trains were obliged to terminate at Ynysybwl station because of the lack of run-round facilities at Old Ynysybwl Platform.

The service on the Nelson branch, following the introduction of the motor cars, comprised 12 trips each way, but evidently this was too generous for the traffic on offer, as by 1907 the timetable had been cut to 10 round trips. The Ynysybwl service was generally 12 cars each way up to World War I. Both branches suffered a temporary reduction in their services in the winter timetable of 1911, when the Nelson line saw a cut to nine trips each way and the Ynysybwl service to only eight each way.

The TVR and its Locomotive Engineer Tom Hurry Riches were clearly very proud of the new motor cars and in December 1904, in an effort to impress others with their performance, the company published details of their operation on the Ynysybwl branch in the railway and other technical press. The costs per mile for operating the cars on the branch were:

Coal, water and stores	1.89*d*.
Wages	2.87*d*.-4.76*d*.

A variety of TVR 0-6-2T engines at Abercynon *c*. 1920.   *LCGB*

Ex-TVR class 'C' 4-4-2T No. 173, as GWR No. 1305, with auto-trailer converted from steam motor car, in the Ynysybwl bay at Pontypridd, *c*. 1922.   *LCGB*

These results were said to compare very favourably with those of the locomotive and coaches previously used.

A third and final batch of motor car locomotive units (Nos. 14-18) and three coach units were delivered to the TVR from Manning, Wardle & Co. of Leeds (locomotive units) and Brush Electrical Engineering Co. of Loughborough (coach units) in 1906. These were of a larger and more powerful type, with accommodation for third class passengers only.

The motor cars used on the Nelson and Ynysybwl services were based at Coke Ovens, Pontypridd, where the engine shed had opened in 1896. A coal stage for use by the cars was authorised by the Traffic Committee on 24th January, 1905, at an estimated cost of £65. On 20th October, 1908, following the annual inspection of the line by the Directors, the Locomotive Committee approved a plan of a proposed motor car shed at Coke Ovens, at an estimated cost of £2,177. In the event the shed was built wider than planned, with an additional expenditure of £1,189 over contract price being authorised on 11th June, 1909. The new shed was a substantial structure, 219 ft. long and covering two lines of rails.

The motor cars were prone to failure, especially as a result of hot axleboxes. A TVR letter, dated 27th November, 1909, records that, by this date, the earlier smaller cars were 'suitable for Ferndale, Nelson and Ynysybwl Branches only'.

Towards the end of 1907 three 'I' class 4-4-0T engines of 1884-5 were fitted with the TVR's decidedly 'Heath Robinson' version of auto-gear and coupled with auto-cars supplied by the Bristol Wagon & Carriage Co. Two auto-sets, each with a engine coupled between two auto-cars, were created, one being used on the Penarth branch and the other on the Pontypridd to Aberthaw service. The third locomotive was kept as spare. Between 1910 and 1912 six 'M1' class 0-6-2T engines were also auto-fitted. In December 1910 two bogie third class carriages, Nos. 331 and 332, were auto-fitted and in 1912 two more auto-trailers were supplied by the Gloucester Railway Carriage & Wagon Co., giving a total of four auto-sets. From 1911 one auto-set was based at Coke Ovens, usually coupled to a 'M1' class 0-6-2T, although 'I' class 4-4-0T engines were also used. This set made appearances on the Nelson and Ynysybwl branches, but the motor cars continued to dominate these services until the end of 1914. From then on the auto-sets took over workings on the Ynysybwl branch, whilst on the Nelson branch the cars were replaced by conventional locomotive and coaches operation. Reflecting these changes, the Ynysybwl branch service remained at 12 workings, each way, daily, whilst by September 1915 the Nelson service was down to only five trains, each way, on weekdays, with an additional four round trips on Saturdays.

In 1916 six 'C' class 4-4-2T engines, dating from 1888 and 1891, were auto-fitted and appeared at Coke Ovens and worked the Ynysybwl branch, together with the earlier auto-fitted types.

The need for wartime economies saw the Ynysybwl service reduced to nine workings, each way, from 13th July, 1917, as part of an overall reduction of 27 per cent in TVR passenger train mileage, following a request for such a cut from the Railway Executive Committee. The service was reduced again in 1918 to only eight round trips. The Nelson branch timetable remained at five trains,

A class '64XX' 0-6-0PT No. 6411 in the Ynysybwl bay at Pontypridd, 11th September, 1951.

H.C. Casserley

Class '57XX' 0-6-0PT No. 4626 stands alongside the coaling stage at Abercynon on 13th July, 1958.

H.C. Casserley

each way, but was increased to six in 1918. Restoration of the Ynysybwl service to its pre-war level came in 1920, with 12 workings each way, but the Nelson branch regained only one extra train each way from this date.

After the Grouping in 1922 ex-TVR locomotives continued to work both branches, with the TVR system of auto-working being retained on the Ynysybwl service. Former class 'I' 4-4-0T engines were extinct by the end of 1925, followed by the ex-class 'C' 4-4-2Ts by 1927. On 1st January, 1926 two auto-fitted ex-class 'M1' 0-6-2T engines, Nos. 492 (ex-TVR No. 180) and 493 (ex-TVR No. 181), were recorded at Coke Ovens Shed and would have appeared on the Ynysybwl branch. Other engines allocated to the shed at this date included a mixed bag of ex-TVR and GWR standard 0-6-2Ts, together with an ex-Barry class 'J' 2-4-2T No. 1316 (ex-ByR No. 91) and ex-Alexandra (Newport & South Wales) Docks & Railway 0-4-2T No. 1426 (ex-A(N&SW)D&R No. 14 purchased from the GWR in 1911). The ex-class 'M1' engines fitted with the TVR system of auto-gear had all been withdrawn by the end of 1928, but from 1926 some of this class were fitted with GWR-type auto-gear, including Nos. 484 (ex-TVR No. 89), 487 (ex-TVR No. 150) and 511 (ex-TVR No. 74), which were at Coke Ovens in January 1926. These conversions had all been withdrawn by the end of 1934.

Two developments brought 'foreign' engines to the Nelson and Ynysybwl branches. Coal traffic was now worked throughout from Lady Windsor Colliery to Barry Docks by engines from Barry Shed, bringing ex-Barry types to the Ynysybwl branch. The iron ore trains from Llanharry to Dowlais were worked as far as Ffaldcaiach by engines from Llantrisant Shed. Standard class '42XX' and '52XX' 2-8-0T engines were permitted to work these trains, provided their speed did not exceed 20 mph at any point, *en route*. Even with this restriction, however, they must have been an impressive sight storming up the 1 in 40 bank above Ynysydwr Junction.

Apart from these workings, the general pattern through the 1920s was for an Abercynon engine to work a daily goods train from Stormstown Junction to Mynachdy Colliery and back, whilst the Nelson branch was covered by a daily goods working, via Cilfynydd, hauled by a Coke Ovens engine. With the transfer of goods traffic to Nelson and Llancaiach station in 1928 this particular working was withdrawn. Cardiff Cathays engines continued to work traffic to and from the Albion Colliery. Dowlais-Cardiff Colliery traffic was worked via Stormstown Junction, rather than via Cilfynydd.

The passenger timetables on both branches remained largely unchanged during the 1920s, with 12 workings each way on the Ynysybwl branch and six on the Nelson line. Auto-working reappeared on the Nelson branch in 1931, covering two early morning services. By this date the branch timetable had been reduced to only four return workings daily, with three extra round trips on Saturdays only. On weekdays the 4.10 pm from Nelson ran through to Llantwit on the Llantrisant branch.

About 1931 'Metro' class 2-4-0T engines were transferred to Coke Ovens from the London area and appeared on the Ynysybwl service. Coke Ovens Shed closed on 31st December, 1933, its allocation, which included 'Metros' Nos. 3595, 3597 and 3599, being transferred to the new shed at Abercynon, which had opened in 1930, having been built on the site of the old TVR shed,

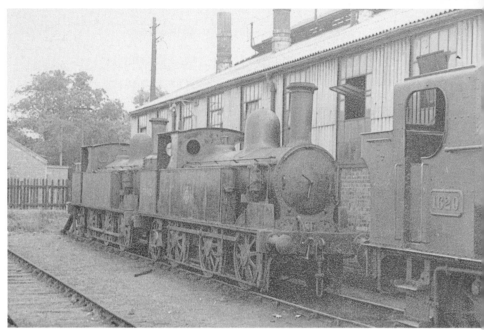

Ex-LNWR 'coal tanks' at Abercynon having been on hire to the National Coal Board for use at Lady Windsor Colliery. *D. Chaplin*

Ex-Barry class 'A' 0-6-0T (ByR No. 2; GWR No. 703) at Lady Windsor Colliery. This engine was sold by the GWR to the Ocean Coal Co. in August 1932 and was scrapped in 1956, still carrying its GWR number. *D. Chaplin*

under the provisions of the Loan and Guarantees Act 1929. In place of the old cramped layout a modern double-track shed 150 feet long had been erected. 'Metro' tanks came to dominate the Ynysybwl auto-trains, but apart from that the mix was very such as before, with ex-TVR and GWR standard 0-6-2T engines providing the staple form of motive power. Gradually, however, with the passage of time and the withdrawal of the older types, the balance swung in favour of the GWR standard classes. The 'Metro' 2-4-0T engines had all gone by the end of 1947, their place having been taken by auto-fitted class '64XX' 0-6-0PT engines, of which Nos. 6401, 6411, 6434 and 6438 were at Abercynon Shed in December 1947. Also shedded there at this time was class '14XX' 0-4-2T No. 1461, which also made appearances on the Ynysybwl auto-service. The last regular passenger working on the branch on 26th July, 1952 was handled by 0-6-0PT No. 5421.

The introduction of diesel locomotives on freight train workings was heralded in late 1961, when 'Hymek' class No. D7012 appeared at Stormstown Junction during trials between Maerdy in the Rhondda Fach Valley and Abercwmboi in the Aberdare Valley. The first of the type which was later to predominate in the valleys of South Wales - the English Electric Type '3' (later class '37') Co-Co diesel electric locomotive - to reach Stormstown Junction was No. D6743, on trial workings on 2nd October, 1962.

Diesel multiple units were introduced on passenger services between Cardiff and Merthyr in 1958. The first known instance of an appearance of one of the new trains on the branches covered by this study was on 11th July, 1959, when a three-car set worked to Ynysybwl and Cilfynydd on an enthusiasts' special organised by the Midlands Area of the Stephenson Locomotive Society. Progress over the branches was extremely sedate, however, as the set was restricted to 5 mph in both cases. The train terminated at the upper junction to the Albion Colliery sidings, at Cilfynydd, and at the former passenger station at Ynysybwl.

Abercynon steam shed closed in November 1964, although it remained in use as a signing-on point for the new diesels, which had arrived earlier in the year. In April 1966 there were five diagrams based at Abercynon, each in the hands of an English Electric Type '3' Co-Co locomotive. One of these (Target No. H34) was responsible for trip working between Lady Windsor Colliery and Stormstown Junction. Another working (Target No. H30) took in Albion Colliery, Cilfynydd, as required. Abercynon ceased to be a signing-on point in 1967, when all train crews were transferred to Radyr.

Merry-go-round working, introduced between Lady Windsor Colliery and Aberthaw Power Stations in the late 1960s, brought Brush Type '4' Co-Co's (later class '47') to the remains of the Ynysybwl branch. One of these trains was involved in one of South Wales' most traditional railway activities - the 'Wild run' - on 14th May, 1968, when, after losing control at Windsor Passing Siding, the train engine and several wagons were derailed at Stormstown Junction.

The class '47' engines later gave way to those of class '37', and it was locomotives of this type which were to enjoy a monopoly of the remaining coal traffic on the line from Lady Windsor Colliery in its final years.

A line up engines, comprising ex-TVR class 'A' 0-6-2Ts Nos. 383 and 373 and ex-GWR class '57XX' 0-6-0PTs Nos. 9769 and 3610 and '64XX' 0-6-0PT No. 6411, at Abercynon on 3rd August, 1957.   *S. Rickard*

Class '57XX' 0-6-0PT No. 3707 outside Abercynon Shed on 13th July, 1958.   *H.C. Casserley*

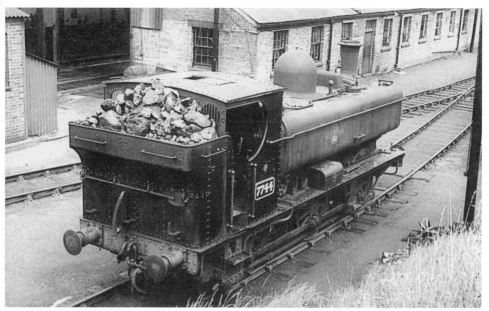

The bunker is piled high with coal on class '57XX' 0-6-0PT No. 7744 at Abercynon Shed yard on 13th July, 1958. *H.C. Casserley*

Passengers from the SLS excursion find much of interest to examine and discuss at Ynysybwl on 11th July, 1959. *S. Rickard*

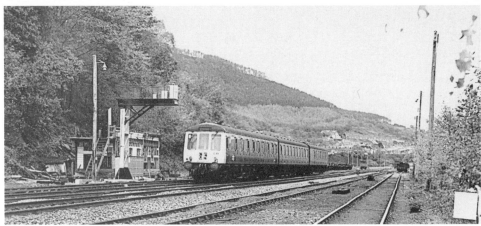

A Merthyr-Barry dmu service passes the remains of Stormstown Junction signal box, 4th November, 1977. *Dr M. Rhodes*

Double-headed English Electric class '37s' Nos. 37 511 and 37 508 are seen on a Lady Windsor Colliery to Aberthaw 'Merry-go-round' train, July 1986. *Dr. M. Rhodes*

Chapter Ten

Epilogue

Following the closure of Lady Windsor Colliery in 1988, traffic ceased on the last part of the complex network of branch lines which had once existed between Pontypridd and Abercynon. All that now remains in use is the former TVR main line between these places. Coal traffic has all but faded away with the closure of local collieries, but there are now two passenger trains each way every hour, following the reopening of the Aberdare branch in 1988. The Glamorgan Rail Strategy, published by Mid and South Glamorgan County Councils in 1985, which formed the basis of many of the later advances in the Valley Lines network, recommended the provision of a new station at Glyncoch, but this particular proposal was not taken any further.

The long-feared incursion via the eastern side of the Taff Valley has come about in a very dramatic fashion with the opening of the A470 trunk road, between Cardiff and Merthyr. This has swept away all traces of the Nelson branch between Coedpenmaen and Ynysydwr Junction. The viaduct over the River Taff, between Pont Shon Norton Junction and Coedpenmaen, remains in place, however, and even carries revenue traffic, if only in the form of an 18 inch water pipe!

The course of the Nelson branch can be followed above Ynysydwr Junction, but at Llanfabon Road the bridge and adjoining earthworks have disappeared. At Nelson the cutting at the station site has been filled in and the land used for a bus station.

Paradoxically, it is the long closed section of the original Llancaiach branch, between Ynysydwr Junction and St Cynon's Church, that retains the strongest presence in the landscape. The route along the hillside, above the Taff Valley, is virtually intact in spite of its last having seen traffic in 1870. The remains of the old inclined plane can still be seen quite clearly from the train, when passing the site of Stormstown Junction.

On the Ynysybwl branch the track to Lady Windsor Colliery is still (in early 1994) largely in place, despite the depredations of vandals and an unscrupulous element of the scrap metal trade, but is now becoming increasingly overgrown.

Ynysybwl station is largely intact, the station building now being used as a surgery. The upper section of the branch can still be traced, with the route of the line from the site of Cwm Siding to the end of the branch being incorporated in a very pleasant country park.

This then is all that remains of the complex network of branch lines, connecting loops and spurs that once existed in and around the Taff Valley between Pontypridd and Abercynon. Gone too is the local coal industry, the principal reason for building the railways in the first place. But the communities which coal and rail brought forth and sustained remain, although now, to their cost, entirely dependent upon other forms of transport.

Appendix One

Principal Acts of Parliament

Nelson Branch

6 Will. IV Cap. lxxxii; 21st June, 1836
Incorporation of TVR;
Railways including Llancaiach branch.

36 & 37 Vict. Cap. clviii; 21st July, 1873
Three railways from TVR to Llancaiach;
Abandonment to part of original Llancaiach branch;

42 & 43 Vict. Cap. cxxxix; 21st July, 1879
Pont Shon Norton branch.

45 & 46 Vict. Cap. cxxxv; 12th July, 1882
Extension of time for railway of 1879 Act.

57 & 58 Vict. Cap. clx; 25th July, 1890
Railway from Pont Shon Norton branch to Coedpenmaen.

59 & 60 Vict. Cap. ccxxxiii; 7th August, 1896
Three railways from Pont Shon Norton branch to Llancaiach branch, Dowlais-Cardiff
Colliery and PC&NR.

Ynysybwl Branch

36 & 37 Vict. Cap. clviii; 21st July, 1873
Two railways from TVR up Clydach Valley.

41 & 42 Vict. Cap. cxliii; 4th July, 1878
Abandonment of south curve at Glyncoch, 1873 Act;
Extension of time for Clydach (or Ynysybwl) branch.

57 & 58 Vict. Cap. clxxii; 17th August, 1894
Clydach Court Loop.

Appendix Two

Summary Biography of George Fisher CE

George Fisher (1809-1891) of the Taff Vale Railway appears in a number of guises in this short work and it may be helpful, at this point, to provide a brief summary of his long and influential career.

c. 1841	Fisher joined the staff of George Bush, Resident Engineer on the construction of the TVR.
September, 1843	Fisher left TVR.
5th November, 1844	Fisher's tender for working the TVR accepted.
23rd December, 1845	Appointed 'Superintendent' of the TVR in place of Mr Highton.
7th January, 1863	Appointed 'Engineer & General Superintendent'.
January, 1867	Redesignated 'Engineer' on appointment of Edwin Page as Traffic Manager.
4th May, 1869	Elected Member of Institute of Civil Engineers.
8th January, 1874	Appointed 'General Manager' on the death of Edwin Page.
13th September, 1883	Appointed 'Resident Director' (i.e. Managing Director), subsequently became Deputy Chairman.
3rd May, 1891	Died at his home at Radyr, near Cardiff.

Acknowledgements

I would like to acknowledge the help of all those who have contributed to the preparation of this book. Special thanks must go to Ray Caston, Derek Chaplin, Tony Cooke, John Dore-Dennis, Eddie Evans, Cliff Harris, Tony Miller, Iorwerth Prothero, Dick Riley, Stephen Rowson and Ian Wright and other members of the Welsh Railways Research Circle, Historical Model Railway Society and Railway & Canal Historical Society, too numerous to mention.

Thanks too, must go to my wife Diana for her forbearance during the research for and preparation of this book.

Bibliography

This book has been compiled almost entirely from primary source material, including company minute books, reports and other documents held at the Public Record Office, Kew, together with contemporary journals and other newspapers. However, the following works have also been consulted:

Locomotive and Train Working in the Latter Part of the 19th Century, E.L. Ahrons, 1923.
The Taff Vale Railway, D.S. Barrie, Oakwood Press, 1962.
The Cowbridge Railway, C. Chapman, Oxford Publishing Co., 1984.
The Llantrisant Branches of the Taff Vale Railway, C. Chapman, Oakwood Press, 1996.
History of the Port of Cardiff, E.L. Chappell, 1939.
Clinker's Register of Closed Stations, C.R. Clinker, Avon Anglia, 1988
Passenger Tramways of Pontypridd, R. Large, Oakwood Press, 1977.
History of the GWR, E.T. MacDermot, GWR, 1927.
The South Wales Coal Industry 1841-1875, J.H. Morris & L.J. Williams, 1958.
GWR Absorbed Coaching Stock 1922/1923, E.R. Mountford, Oakwood Press, 1978.
The Locomotives of the GWR (Part 10), RCTS, 1966.
Top Sawyer - A Biography of David Davies of Llandinam, I. Thomas, 1988.

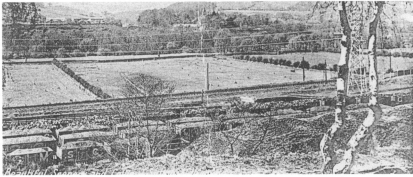

Looking west from Cilfynydd across the colliery sidings and part of the goods yard, *c.* 1910. *Pontypridd Library*